TRAUMA
&
Transformation

For Mary Lynne, Eliza, and Mary Laura. The joys of my life.
L. G. C.

For Joan, Michael, and my parents, for all they have given.
R. G. T.

TRAUMA
&
Transformation

Growing in the
Aftermath of Suffering

Richard G. Tedeschi
Lawrence G. Calhoun

SAGE Publications
International Educational and Professional Publisher
Thousand Oaks   London   New Delhi

For information address:

SAGE Publications, Inc.
2455 Teller Road
Thousand Oaks, California 91320
E-mail: order@sagepub.com

SAGE Publications Ltd.
6 Bonhill Street
London EC2A 4PU
United Kingdom

SAGE Publications India Pvt. Ltd.
M-32 Market
Greater Kailash I
New Delhi 110 048 India

Printed in the United States of America

Library of Congress Cataloging-in-Publication Data

Tedeschi, Richard G.
   Trauma and transformation: Growing in the aftermath of suffering
/ Richard G. Tedeschi, Lawrence G. Calhoun.
      p.   cm.
   Includes bibliographical references and index.
   ISBN 0-8039-5256-2 (alk. paper).—ISBN 0-8039-5257-0 (pbk.:
alk. paper)
   1. Suffering.   2. Life change events—Psychological aspects.
   3. Adjustment (Psychology)   4. Self-actualization (Psychology)
I. Title.
BF789.S8T   1995
155.9'3—dc20   95-11803

This book is printed on acid-free paper.

95 96 97 98 99   10 9 8 7 6 5 4 3 2 1

Sage Production Editor: Tricia K. Bennett
Sage Typesetter: Andrea D. Swanson
Cover Illustration: Dawn Anderson

CONTENTS

PREFACE

This volume is an attempt to weave together material from various writings in philosophy, religion, and especially psychology to account for a phenomenon that has been recognized since ancient times but given little attention by psychologists: the experience of personal growth or strengthening that often occurs in persons who have faced traumatic events. We use an essentially cognitive framework to explain this experience because changes in belief systems seem to be so often reported by persons who describe their growth, and these beliefs appear to play a central role in relieving emotional distress and encouraging useful activity.

Although both of us have experienced traumatic events in our lives, we are personally unfamiliar with many of the events mentioned in this book. Our teachers have been the clients with whom we have worked as clinicians, and the people who have agreed to talk with us, sometimes for hours, as part of our research studies in this area. It is to these people we owe the greatest debt. They have not only informed us as psychologists, but made us more sensitive to the struggles and victories of those who have been most painfully touched by life.

We hope that we have presented information in a way that is accessible to clinicians, laypersons, and especially in Chapter 9, other people who have experienced trauma. We have also tried to summarize a far-flung literature and describe a way of understanding the process of growth that will encourage more attention from researchers. In addition, we believe that this book can be used as a supplementary

text in courses on human development, crisis intervention, and intro-
ductory courses in counseling and psychotherapy. It is also our hope
that this book will be useful as a resource for helping professionals in
a variety of disciplines, including psychology, social work, psychiatry,
family counseling, human services, nursing, and sociology.

We wish to acknowledge the assistance of Arnie Cann, Lori Folk,
Carl Frye, Donna Harding, and the other students and colleagues with
whom we have the pleasure to work. We thank Raymond Berger for
his helpful and incisive review of our manuscript. We are especially
grateful for the reassignment of duties granted to the senior author by
the University of North Carolina at Charlotte. This greatly facilitated
the completion of this project. Finally, we express our appreciation to
our editors at Sage, Marquita Flemming and Jim Nageotte, for sup-
porting our work.

Richard G. Tedeschi
Lawrence G. Calhoun
Charlotte, North Carolina

THE USES OF SUFFERING

Religious and Psychological Roots

But we also boast in our sufferings, knowing that suffering produces endurance, and endurance produces character, and character produces hope, and hope does not disappoint us.

—Romans 5:5

Jerry is a 34-year-old paraplegic man who has been disabled for 8 years following an automobile accident. Most able-bodied people would assume that this was the most traumatic[1] event of this man's life. But Jerry sees it differently.

> This was the one thing that happened in my life that I needed to have happen; it was probably the best thing that ever happened to me. On the outside looking in that's pretty hard to swallow, I'm sure, but hey, that's the way I view it. If I hadn't experienced this and lived through it, I likely wouldn't be here today because of my lifestyle previously—I was on a real self-destructive path. If I had it to do all over again, I would want it to happen the same way. I would not want it not to happen.

Jerry is certainly correct when he says this viewpoint is hard for most people to accept. But researchers are discovering that this is precisely the approach to life trauma that many people adopt. Even if

1

they do not always state that, in hindsight, they are pleased the traumatic event occurred, many people at least view the aftermath of the event as something that has benefited them. Furthermore, the people who take this point of view feel that they have made a very satisfactory adjustment, and to the outside world they may even appear inspirational. For example, in her autobiography, Helen Keller speaks of her teacher's dedication to her: "So I say my education was accomplished in the tragedy of my teacher's life. She understood the void in my soul because her childhood had been so empty of joy" (Keller, 1968, p. 346).

We have been interested in learning more about these people and this remarkable process of strengthening that may occur when they confront tragedies in their lives. There is nothing new or remarkable in the assertion that psychological growth can be precipitated by the pain of unfortunate events. What we have found new and remarkable is how often this happens and how apparently ordinary people achieve extraordinary wisdom through their struggle with circumstances that are initially aversive in the extreme. We have also developed some principles that we believe explain the process by which the struggle is successfully resolved and this wisdom is attained. First, we will consider briefly some of the accumulated wisdom about trauma and suffering and how approaching these aspects of life in certain ways leads to the strength to persevere and insight into why it is worthwhile to do so.

Tragedy in Philosophy and Literature

From the time of the ancient Greeks to the present day, tragedy has been a dominant theme in great literary works. The enduring popularity of this literature has prompted authors, philosophers, and literary critics to ponder what continues to attract people to tragic themes, and somehow to enjoy observing the human struggle with the tragic through literature. Aristotle addresses the importance of this literature in his *Poetics*. He defines tragedy very broadly as sad or serious stories, but also describes the best kind, where a good but flawed man commits an immoral deed, only recognizing later what he has done (Kelly, 1993). The hero's remorse provides a catharsis that is purifying, and perhaps therapeutic for the spectator (Aristotle, 1970). These tragic figures become their best selves, enlarged (Rorty, 1992). Hegel (Paolucci & Paolucci, 1962) wrote extensively on tragedy, which for him is the conflict and action of the tragic figure that produces his eventual suffering—mere suffering alone is not truly tragic. He also concluded that "reconciliation" with the gods is the best conclusion for tragedy. By witnessing the drama, the viewer is also transformed by the recognition of his or her connection to the tragic figures.

Of course, tragedy presented as art gives an aesthetic pleasure not gained in real-life tragedy. In the literature of tragedy, our pity for the hero is combined with admiration, whereas in life, we are likely only to pity those enduring tragedy (Raphael, 1960). When we consider the reactions of the involved audience for tragedy, we recognize that there is a *felt* knowledge that is gained through the "immediacy and physicality of tragic drama" (Berlin, 1981, p. 174), which is a reflection of life's mystery. Confrontation with the mystery is what occurs in this involved audience and with the individual who is involved in the struggle of suffering. The hero is on the brink of the abyss—what is unknown and incomprehensible—and this is the situation confronted by those facing crises. When these crises occur, we are given the opportunity, and are forced, to confront the most threatening questions that are always there, but hidden. Berlin (1981) terms this the "secret cause"—what is behind the play and verified by our life experience.

Therefore, we have good reason to seek out the next best thing to real suffering, and that is its representation in a vivid, accessible form in tragic literature. Because people living through crisis cannot give an effective running commentary, the characters of drama, given words by the dramatist, overcome this limitation (Schier, 1983). If we ourselves suffer, we must find our own words for this experience and the way the experience illuminates life's mystery, thus enabling us to benefit from it as the audience may benefit from the performance of tragedy. We can find some connection between what is learned by the readers of tragic literature and the victims of tragedy in life if we consider what can be learned from both these experiences.

Krook (1969) described four universal elements of tragedy that illuminate the relationship of tragedy as explored in literature to the focus of this book on individual growth as a result of trauma. The first element of tragedy is the act of shame or horror that precipitates the suffering. The *precipitant* may be set in motion by the tragic hero, intended or only imagined, although, according to Krook, in all cases these tragic circumstances arise from the fundamental nature of humans. Not all life crises can be subjects of such tragedy, according to these criteria. The second element of tragedy, *suffering*, is "properly tragic if and only if it generates knowledge, in the sense of insight into, understanding of, man's fundamental nature or the fundamental human condition" (Krook, 1969, p. 8). This *knowledge* is the third element of tragedy. In turn, this knowledge is tragic to the extent that it provides an affirmation of the worthwhile nature of human life and the dignity of the human spirit. This *affirmation* is the final element of tragedy.

These final three elements are closely related to the consequences of the struggle in which people engage as they cope with life crises. Krook describes the knowledge gained as simple and self-explanatory, and it is felt intensely, genuinely, and sincerely. However, this knowledge may or may not be self-knowledge. It may instead be universal. Therefore, although the tragic hero may not gain knowledge, the readers or audience receive this knowledge through their "God's-eye view" (Raphael, 1960). In Athenian tragedy, this universal knowledge was shared by the members of the community who attended the theater, so that traumatized soldiers could heal and all could cherish mortality and personal attachments in the face of the losses of war (Shay, 1994). This knowledge reveals things about life that produce a sense of affirmation in spite of the suffering. Again, we will see that this appears to be an important element in the individual experience of people who are traumatized by life events but who accomplish psychological growth.

What is ultimately affirmed for some people who grow through their trauma is that there is an objective, transcendent moral order that reaches beyond the individual and even humanity. According to Krook (1969), this illumination comes with the recognition and acceptance that suffering is necessary. In people suffering life crises, the events producing the suffering may not be viewed as necessary, but the suffering, the struggle, can be viewed as necessary to gain the valuable knowledge and affirmation that succeeds it. Hence, a person such as Jerry, described at the outset, can come to see the event and its consequent suffering as not only necessary but desirable.

People show a persistent interest in literary tragedy and religious study, indicating enduring concern with the most troubling issues of the human condition. But reading tragedy or attending a performance of it allows us to be in the position of learning the lessons without the pain, and in this way we have a very different experience from people who may be profoundly changed in a positive way by adversity. People experiencing crises have the good fortune to be put in a position in which their misfortune is a classroom for learning these things in the most intense, genuine way. Kierkegaard (1983) wrote that these experiences of crisis were necessary for full personal development. Schopenhauer (1942) sees boredom as the price to be paid if we somehow avoid pain. As Krook (1969) stated in referring to the literature of tragedy, the lessons reach beyond the individual and speak to the existential issues, providing an affirmation for living. But there are other viewpoints on this. For example, Nietzsche (1955) warns that "spiritual arrogance" (p. 220) can come from suffering deeply, when people believe that the knowledge gained through suffering is beyond that of the wisest people.

Religious Views of Suffering

There is a tradition in religious and philosophical writings that supports the notion that the greatest and wisest have suffered turmoil in their explorations of meaning that may be concealed in the most trying circumstances. Little (1989) points out that it is inconceivable to consider religion apart from suffering, and that each religion faces the difficulty of producing a consistent and satisfying explanation of it. He has provided a categorization scheme for the themes of suffering found in the Eastern and Western theological literature, including four types of legitimate suffering: retributive suffering, therapeutic suffering, pedagogical suffering, and vicarious suffering.

In considering Judaic and Christian explanations of suffering, Little sees all four types of legitimate suffering represented. Especially in the Old Testament and the rewards and punishments to come in the Last Judgment, the retributive notion of "an eye for an eye" is commonplace. But other themes of suffering are present in the Judeo-Christian tradition that can provide a vehicle for renewal. In a discussion of doxology, Brueggemann (1984) notes that the book of Psalms was written in a stylized fashion expressing continuing faith in the face of misery. He notes that the people of Israel do not try ad hoc to make faith affirmations out of private experience. Instead, in times of struggle, Israel returns to the traditional formulations that seem to have special credibility in difficult times. The Psalms continue to provide an alternative, "especially in a time of 'subjective consciousness' as ours, which wants always to find 'meaning' through personal feeling and inclination. Israel knew another way made available in this stylized speech" (Brueggemann, 1984, pp. 61-62).

In the rabbinic period, suffering was viewed as a test, and in the control of God. Indeed, it is one of the blessings bestowed by God to draw people close to Him. People are encouraged to look for suffering as an opportunity for advancement (Bowker, 1970), as well as a way of atonement. This understanding of suffering as a means of grace for all of the faithful allowed the Jews to endure persecution. In the trials of the biblical figure Job, painful experiences serve as messages from God. Adversity has been viewed as including messages that cause people to reflect on why they suffer. Sickness has been viewed as a type of suffering that removes people from material pursuits, so that time is available for quiet reflection. Moral lapses resulting in rejection from others can prompt people to reconsider their behavior and ponder eternal values (Singer, 1964).

Little's (1989) categories of suffering can be seen in the Christian faith. The suffering of Christ, especially because it was undeserved, provides a counterpoint to retributive suffering. The events of Christ's life, death, and resurrection cannot be erased by any experience of suffering, and this can have a healing or therapeutic effect for the sufferer. Whenever God's will is made clearer as a result of suffering, a pedagogical element is present as well.

> Every tribulation is a medicine or blessing in disguise, provided men accept and use it in the right spirit. This is so because God sends tribulation either to inspire us to repentance for past sin; or to prevent us from falling into potential sin; or to test our patience. (Miles, 1965, p. 25)

An important distinction is made by writers who note that life's difficulties, although they may bring us closer to God and promote a struggle that fosters wisdom, are not the doing of God. We need to look honestly at these miseries. "Paul didn't call his misery 'a blessing in disguise.' He didn't spray it with perfume so as to make it smell like a rose. He says: 'A thorn was given to me in the flesh, a messenger from Satan, to harass me from being too elated!' " (Hoyt, 1978, p. 76).

This distinction will be an important one that we will pursue later in this book as we discuss the possibility that some people create a perception of benefits that may allow them to transcend the continuing pain of their difficult life circumstance. Paul confronted his pain and was told by God, "My grace is sufficient for you, for my power is made perfect in weakness" (Hoyt, 1978, p. 77). These miseries have been viewed as necessary for spiritual growth. "It is not peace of mind that brings us to wholeness, but struggle and conflict, and spiritual enlightenment occurs only when a person has been through dark and disturbing trials of the soul" (Sanford, 1977, p. 20).

From this perspective, the spiritual growth that comes with suffering is reflected in the actions of the person and in the impact that a person can have on others. The experience of this struggle produces a wisdom and inspiration that could not otherwise be achieved. Suffering keeps us humble and patient, not knowing why we suffer until we know the will of God. Just as was evident in the descriptions of the value of tragic literature mentioned above, in the Christian perspective, the opportunity to suffer should be welcomed because it is the only path to wisdom and strength. If we don't know suffering, we remain shallow. "Suffering, on the other hand, tends to plow up the surface of our lives to uncover the depths that provide greater strength of purpose and accomplishment. Only deeply plowed earth can yield bountiful harvests" (Graham, 1981, p. 27). Suffering is discipline that produces a deepening of the spiritual life. "Have you ever considered that steel is iron plus fire; soil is rock plus crushing; linen is flax plus the comb that separates, and the flail that pounds, and the shuttle that weaves!" (Graham, 1981, p. 85). Renewal is not possible without struggle in this perspective. To know life profoundly requires times of testing, and life involves continuous struggle.

New life is never a gift in a vacuum. It is wrought in profound and dangerous struggle as we bring to visibility the deep incongruity that marks our life. Our life is one in which all that is finally holy is violated,

day by day. Yet, we dare hope for pastoral possibilities that move us beyond
the wrenching, venomous indignation. (Brueggemann, 1984, p. 74)

There are three potential strengths that we must rely on to accomplish
this: God, our will, and the lives of others. In relying on these strengths,
we develop an "internal capacity to cope, or better still, to transform the
tragic experiences into creative encounters with life" (Thomas, 1978, p. 20).
Notice that a distinction is made between *coping* and *transformation*. This
distinction will be part of our description of responses to trauma and is
crucial to the thesis of this book: that some people do not merely cope
with trauma, but are transformed by the struggle with it. In the writings
about the Christian perspective on tragedy and suffering, the idea appears that "Christianity transmutes the tragedy of history into something
which is not tragedy" (Niebuhr, 1937, p. 193). We can apply this to the
individual's history as well as human history. The person who is able to
accomplish this transmutation of the tragedies of personal life comes to
understand life in a more profound way. For Christians, this understanding comes through discipleship and identification with Christ,
making suffering welcome.

Other great religions also view suffering as having salutary effects.
Some elements of Islam contain the theme of welcoming suffering,
particularly in the Shiite tradition. Consider a passion play in which
the seventh-century martyr Husain, about to be killed, states: "Trials,
afflictions, and pains, the thicker they fall on man, the better, dear
sister, do they prepare him for his journey heavenward" (Bowker,
1970, pp. 131-132). Suffering is seen as instrumental in the purposes
of God. In Buddhism, "essential to progress in wisdom is developing
the understanding of the universality of suffering" (Little, 1989, p. 68).
This is accomplished in the Buddhist tradition by confronting suffering directly, conquering suffering by embracing it. For example, Bud-
dha's Noble Truths are the way his teaching is organized around the
issue of suffering. Suffering appears to be universal and inescapable,
and the causes of this suffering must be removed by ethical and
compassionate action. Therefore, suffering is to be approached rather
than avoided. The self-immolation of Buddhist monks in Vietnam in
1963 used individual suffering to prove the importance of the message
that Vietnam was suffering by saying it with the greatest sincerity and
courage (Bowker, 1970).

Although Hinduism is often thought to be unconcerned with suffering in this life because of the emphasis on individual salvation, the issue of suffering plays a key role because it is viewed as a result of actions in former incarnations. The challenge in living then becomes the balancing of detachment and involvement in response to the suffering with which an individual is confronted in order to fulfill the duties appropriate to one's stage of life and caste. A passage from the Mahabharata Santiparva states that "happiness and misery, prosperity and adversity, gain and loss, death and life, in their turn, wait upon all creatures. For this reason the wise man of tranquil self would neither be elated with joy nor be depressed with sorrow" (Bowker, 1970, p. 224). Cultivation of an even disposition is necessary because suffering and happiness are transitory. Recognition that happiness ends in sorrow and that happiness sometimes arises out of sorrow promotes the wise approach to living.

Referring to Little's (1989) scheme, we are most concerned in this book with the tendency of many people to identify the therapeutic and pedagogical elements in their suffering whether or not they are religious. Although the world's great religious traditions to some extent embody this tendency, it is unclear whether people tend to identify the therapeutic and pedagogical significance of suffering because of the influence of religion, or because this reflects "something deep and abiding in the human mind and heart" (Little, 1989, p. 71).

It is important to recognize that people profit not from the adversity itself, nor from the achievement and success that might result. "The fruit of wisdom is not in the solution of mysteries, but in knowing how to live best under life's difficulties and uncertainties" (Scott, 1971, pp. 186-187). An important element in the struggle with life's difficulties is the acceptance of limitations. Later, we will include this element in our description of both the process by which a transformation becomes possible during the struggle with trauma and the wisdom that accrues from it. Any "attempts to transcend the limits of mortal existence through struggle or through wisdom are doomed to failure. Therefore it is part of wisdom to accept life with serenity and courage, and so to find its hidden treasure" (Scott, 1971, p. 186). Such themes find echoes in the writings of existential philosophers and especially existential psychologists.

Psychological Views of Suffering

The perspective of existentialist philosophers, that wisdom was the recognition of the absurdity and meaninglessness of life, was altered as the existential approach was applied to psychology, and especially to the needs of individuals attempting to find meaning in the midst of life struggles. Existential psychologists define destiny as the "givens" in life that must be accepted, and within these constraints we exercise our freedom to choose a life path (May, 1981). We cannot make any change we wish, but we can choose how we will respond to the conditions of our lives, from the fact that we will someday die, to the acts of other people or nature that impinge on us moment to moment. Life becomes meaningful through our confrontation with our choices within our destiny.

Victor Frankl may be the best known of the psychologists to address suffering from this existential perspective. Despair was not viewed as the direct product of suffering but as the consequence of suffering that was viewed as having no meaning (Frankl, 1961). Frankl points out that people cannot find meaning in their existence merely through creative acts and existential encounters, but must confront what he terms the "primordial facts" of existence: suffering, guilt, and transitoriness. By engaging in a confrontation with these, a person has an opportunity to develop through the process of finding meaning.

Similar existential human dilemmas are described by Erich Fromm (1947). Inherent in each is a recognition of our isolation and mortality, and we seek to allay our fears of these. Through attempts to meet existential needs, we ward off insanity and go beyond this to reunite with the world in a productive fashion in which one's individuality is expressed through love and work. This psychological growth comes about only because the individual faces squarely the inescapable tragedies of life: the necessity of choice, isolation, and death.

In existential psychology, growth, often termed individuation or self-actualization, comes as the inherent difficulties of life are sought out and confronted as opportunities to learn the most profound meanings of being human.

> Individuation is a work, a life opus, a task that calls upon us not to avoid life's difficulties and dangers, but to perceive the meaning in the pattern

of events that form our lives. . . . It does not necessarily mean happiness, but growth. It is often painful, but, fortunately, it is never boring. It is not getting out of life what we think we want, but it is the development and purification of the soul. (Sanford, 1977, p. 20)

Unwelcome traumatic events may provide similar opportunities, even in those people not otherwise aware of the search for answers to these large issues of living. When traumas are addressed through confrontation with them, constructive living and psychological growth are possible. People can adopt an attitude toward their suffering that allows it to cease to be *mere* suffering. Instead, traumatic events can be made to have meaning and be an opportunity for growth (Averill & Nunley, 1992). This involves a changed perspective.

I began to see that in the deepest experiences the human being can know—the birth of a baby, the prolonged illness or death of a loved relative, the loss of a job, the creation of a poem, a painting, a symphony, the grief of a fire, a flood, an accident—each in its own way . . . brings into awareness new dimensions of self, new beauty, new power for human compassion, and a reverence for the precious nature of each breathing moment. (Moustakas, 1961, p. 7)

It also involves action. Consider the response of a man who lost all his belongings in a house fire. Because of his subsequent anger, he then lost his job. The man recounted this as the "most difficult, but in the long run the most beneficial time of [his] life" (Averill & Nunley, 1992, p. 200) because it prompted him to try something he had always been afraid to do: start his own business. He was successful, and he found a new way of seeing himself. "I realized I had the courage to face almost anything . . . a combined sense of courage and pride in myself. A new feeling for me" (p. 200).

An important distinction should also be considered between the physical and the psychological nature of suffering in order to make sense of the approach to this issue, which assumes that a relief of suffering may be defined as absence of pain or the end of a situation that promotes suffering. Although pain is a physiological phenomenon, suffering is a psychological one, and relief of suffering may be much more achievable than relief of pain or the curing of an illness (Abrams, 1989). For example, in a project where severely physically handicapped young people moved from a nursing home to community living, one resident stated, "This could be everything from a dream come true to a slum situation. It's all in how you want to view this. Some days I come here and I think it's a slum" (Anderson, 1989, p. 115). If suffering is essentially nonphysical in nature, psychological or spiritual routes to overcoming it become available. Within the Hindu tradition, one can cultivate a greater and greater detachment from one's own suffering, and thereby come to the recognition that suffering is eliminated when its ultimate falseness is recognized. Such changes in perspective may be crucial in any person who is successfully alleviating his or her own suffering and moving toward some perception of benefit from it. Especially important is the recognition and distinction made between unchangeable aspects of the difficult events and the ways that acting or even thinking differently about these events brings relief and positive personal change.

In writing about the psychological effects of chronic pain, Leder (1984-1985) states that the experience of inescapable pain deconstructs what we have known about our world, ultimately defeating all attempts at interpretation, making it all seem senseless. Even after physical suffering has passed, this meaninglessness can always reemerge into our awareness because we are always aware of having suffered. Leder sees no important distinction between the experience of emotional and physical pain because both have physical and emotional elements. Furthermore, "precisely as a primordially negative event, pain can take on a range of positive significances" (Leder, 1984-1985, p. 262). Our alienation from our bodies when we are in pain makes clearer the mind-body dualism, producing the therapeutic effect of the recognition that suffering is temporary. The experience of pain produces the most far-reaching searches for meaning among the paradoxes that pain reveals: dependency on others for relief versus the loneliness of our private experience, especially when others' help does not cure; the search for relief by not daring to move or by engaging in activity; the fact that pain focuses us inward yet external distractions often help.

Beyond the recognition among psychologists that there are opportunities for psychological growth in trauma and suffering, there is also the viewpoint, similar to that expressed in literature and religion, that for the individual to achieve the greatest psychological health, some kind of suffering is *necessary*. Shostrom (1976), an existential psychotherapist, has stated that "most people who become self-actualizing do so as a result of a struggle to overcome problems in their lives" (p. 311). It is evident that religious, literary, and psychological descriptions of coping with crisis all contain elements of the idea that gains can be made beyond restoration of psychological and spiritual equilibrium as a result of engaging suffering, and that struggling through life crises may be the only route to wisdom and the highest form of living.

Plan for This Book

In this book, we will attempt to understand this apparently mystical process from a contemporary psychological perspective. The approach will be used to illuminate and integrate aspects of the experience of people struggling with crises into a description of the coping process, and to suggest ways in which survivors of trauma, their caretakers, and professionals can encourage not only successful coping but also beneficial life changes. We will examine in detail the abilities and characteristics of people who derive some benefits from negative events, and we will examine the kinds of events that are more likely to produce substantial benefits over the long run, as perceived by survivors. We will describe ways in which these factors may interact so that certain people are more likely to derive benefits from certain kinds of events. We will also look at the issue of the meaning that people find in struggling with these crises, and what appropriate role professionals and caregivers can play in encouraging the process of psychological growth in people experiencing suffering. First, however, it is important to consider the traditional research literature on the psychological aftermath of life trauma. Before proceeding with the general examination of the growth that occurs in the struggle with tragedy, we will first look at this research literature that has been focused on the negative and difficult aspects of life crises.

Note

1. We recognize that theorists and clinicians have often drawn distinctions between the terms *trauma* and *crisis*. We will be using these terms interchangeably to mean sets of circumstances that seriously challenge or overwhelm an individual's capacity to cope.

THE NEGATIVE
CONSEQUENCES OF TRAUMA

If it were not for my loyalty to God and my friends, I'd wish to die.
—Reinhold Niebuhr, in pain at the end of his life

At the age of 24, Charles had a bright future. As a third-year medical student, he was nearing completion of an exciting, demanding program of study. Although as an undergraduate student he had experienced some lack of vocational direction, late in his junior year he discovered his interest in medicine. He promptly altered his program of study, joined the pre-med club sponsored by the biology department at his school, and began the process of seeking admission to professional school. After his enrollment in medical school, he lost any doubts he might have had about his career choice—he had really found his niche. His course performance and the feedback he obtained from the medical school faculty told him he would be a very successful physician.

Charles's good life was shaken in the fall of his fourth year in medical school. His only sister, 3 years younger than he, was diagnosed as having incurable liver cancer and died within 2 weeks of the diagnosis. Two months later, Charles's father, a prominent psychiatrist, took his own life. The loss of his only daughter was too heavy a burden for him. Charles's life seemed changed forever by these swift and terrible losses.

Like Jerry, whom we met in the previous chapter, Charles is just one of us. Every day, in all parts of the world, individuals face such life traumas: a disaster that causes tragic loss of life, a hurricane that devastates a whole community, the spread of the AIDS virus, or the diagnosis of a terminal illness in a close friend. We also face major challenges that may not be as widespread or dramatic, but nevertheless strain our ability to keep going—a spouse confesses to extramarital affairs, a child is injured in a school bus wreck, an infant develops a serious medical problem, or a company is purchased and middle-aged employees are fired. What happens psychologically to people facing these negative events?

In Chapter 1, we showed that our religious and philosophical traditions have suggested that difficult life events could contain the seeds for psychological and spiritual growth. Jerry's experience clearly illustrates how individuals can change and grow from the struggle with difficult events. It is clear, however, that good outcomes are not the first things that come to mind when we consider tragic life events. Before we examine the research findings on the positive aspects of trauma, we turn our attention in this chapter to the negative impact that major traumas can have on psychological functioning. In Charles Dickens's phrase, this chapter looks at how life trauma can, for many people, be "the worst of times." We will turn our attention first to the characteristics of life events that make them traumatic.

What Makes Events Traumatic?

What qualities of the crises we face are likely to foreshadow negative psychological consequences? Focusing on the circumstances themselves, what makes a particular event into a trauma?

The word "trauma" itself indicates that an event is a shock. When challenges occur *suddenly and unexpectedly,* they are more likely to threaten our psychological well-being (McCann & Pearlman, 1990; Weiss & Parkes, 1983). This is not to say that critical life problems that happen gradually and are expected cannot be highly stressful—they can. However, it is harder to achieve a resolution under very difficult circumstances when there is insufficient time to prepare ourselves psychologically.

Charles had very little time to prepare for his sister's death, and his father's suicide came without warning. Although both of these sad losses would be difficult even with warning, they are likely to have presented Charles with significantly greater challenges because they occurred as a shock to him.

Another quality of events that makes them traumatic is *perceived lack of control* over them (Slaby, 1989; Tennen & Affleck, 1990). Most of the tragedies that befall us are not under our control. Major illness, loss of loved ones, economic hardship, natural disasters, and similar difficulties cannot be directly controlled. Although these events have consequences that are direct in their impact (e.g., loss of a place to live), their uncontrollable nature adds to the likelihood that they will have a negative impact on people who are exposed to them. Even if we have a general belief that we can make changes in much of what happens to us, the overwhelmingly clear impossibility of reversing such events as the death of a loved one, the devastation caused by killer tornadoes, or the crash of the stock market makes events such as these particularly traumatic for most of us. Events that cause us to experience powerlessness are more likely to challenge our psychological well-being.

Events that are *out of the ordinary* are likely to be more difficult for us to handle (McCann & Pearlman, 1990). In part, this may be because unusual events are also likely to be sudden and out of our control. But also, we cannot bring our experience to bear on unfamiliar events. In addition, individuals who can help with events that are familiar to all of us may not know how to help when the circumstances lack familiarity. For example, although others may have had ideas about how to provide support to Charles when his sister died from liver cancer, they may have been more hesitant about what to do on the occasion of his father's suicidal death (Calhoun & Allen, 1991).

Another quality that makes an event traumatic is the *degree to which it creates long-lasting problems* (Davidson, Fleming, & Baum, 1986). Many of the minor problems in life are easily reversible. If a student fails a course, the course can be repeated. If spouses have an argument, they can make up. If you have a summer cold, you will soon recover. But an accident that produces irreversible paraplegia will create problems that will not go away. The need to use different modes of transportation, the need to negotiate physical barriers, and the prejudice many people with disabilities face will never completely disappear. Life circumstances that create difficulties that stay with us will be more likely to lead to significant psychological distress. In part, this distress may be due to the sense of hopelessness that is produced when certain events are acknowledged to be irreversible and unchangeable. For example, parents who lose an infant child may accept the inevitability of things never being the same again. Although they may, at some time, be less depressed about their loss, they may miss the child for the rest of their lives.

Irreversible changes can produce a great lack of control and reveal few opportunities to take direct, corrective action. It may be easy for people in such difficult situations to learn to feel helpless and become depressed. An unchanged negative situation can evoke these emotions at any time the situation is recalled, even when it occurred long ago. For example, people who have suffered bereavement or permanent disability may be inevitably and consistently confronted with the reality of loss. They are required to adjust and accept, rather than to work to reverse these situations.

Another quality that makes an event traumatic is *blame.* Common sense suggests that individuals who experience a highly negative event are likely to feel better about their situation if they do *not* blame themselves for what happened. In fact, the reverse may be the case (Tennen & Affleck, 1990). Trauma survivors often ask themselves, "Did I do something to cause this or was this somebody else's fault?" Current research (Downey, Silver, & Wortman, 1990; Tennen & Affleck, 1990) indicates that people who blame others for their difficult circumstances are likely to have more psychological difficulties than are people who do not. On the surface, this seems unreasonable. But blaming others can be a sign that a person feels powerless over the circumstances. To the extent that blaming others increases the individual's sense of helplessness (Abrahamson, Metalsky, & Alloy, 1989), psychological distress resulting from the event can be expected.

Finally, we should consider the varying *impact of particular crises at different times in the life cycle.* The consequences of an event occurring in adulthood may be different from those of a childhood crisis. Because it appears that personal identity is established fairly clearly by late adolescence, crises that occur during adulthood will be a threat to an already established identity, whereas those experienced during childhood are more likely to be integrated into an identity that is then carried throughout life, representing the basis for thinking, perceiving, and reacting to life situations. For example, growing up with a physical disability is likely to produce a different psychological reaction from experiencing the disability later in life—after emotional investments have already been made in an identity as an able-bodied person. It is also likely that abuse suffered during childhood will mean something different from the same abuse suffered as an adult. We can expect that one's initial understanding of and reaction to the event, the degree of threat to established personal identity, the degree to which the event and its consequences are integrated into identity, the meaning of the event, and adaptive capabilities all will depend, to some extent, on when in the life cycle the trauma occurs.

We have suggested that traumatic events that are sudden and unexpected, uncontrollable, out of the ordinary, chronic, and are blamed on others are more likely to produce psychological difficulties for the individual who has experienced them. We will now address what those difficulties might be.

The Negative Impact of Traumatic Events

The brief description of Charles's tragic circumstances at the beginning of the chapter did not elaborate on how Charles reacted to them. Both professionals and laypersons, however, are likely to predict that Charles has a high likelihood of experiencing significant levels of distress, perhaps even developing a psychiatric problem. There are thousands of studies on how stressful events can produce negative consequences for the individuals who are exposed to them. Although our main focus in this book is on the ways in which major trauma can lead to psychological growth, it would be naive to suggest that highly negative events do not have highly negative consequences—they do. It is therefore appropriate to examine some of the ways in which critical life problems cause significant difficulties. We will look at the negative impact of traumatic events in two general areas: negative psychological effects and negative physical effects.

NEGATIVE PSYCHOLOGICAL EFFECTS

In what ways can highly stressful events negatively affect the individual? The focus here is not on evaluating the risk of psychiatric disorders (we will address that issue later), but on describing responses that many people have to traumatic events.

Effects on Thoughts

Particularly when the event is sudden and unexpected, initial reactions of shock, disbelief, and psychological numbness are not uncommon (Calhoun & Atkeson, 1991; Davis & Friedman, 1985; Raphael, 1986). One client described it with these words—"It was like I had been given a big shot of psychological Novocain. I couldn't feel *anything.*" For most people, however, the "psychological Novocain" does not provide complete protection from the unpleasant circumstances. Related to this are experiences of acting automatically, without being able to think except in the most narrow, focused terms. One man whose wife wished to divorce him described himself as a "zombie" while at his attorney's office, signing the separation papers. His only thought was that he needed to see his daughter as soon as possible.

For many, the traumatic events intrude into their thoughts. Thoughts, images, and recollections of the event break into consciousness with disturbing regularity. These come unbidden and unwanted. For example, bereaved parents often report being caught off guard by recollections of their child prompted by innocuous cues such as a toy, a song, or a holiday. The intrusions may also happen during sleep, in the form of nightmares about the event or about related circumstances (Adler, 1943; Wilkinson, 1983; Wilson, 1989). For example, an emergency room physician (who had a 2-year-old son), after caring for three preschool children critically injured in an automobile wreck, began to have dreams about children crying. The cries were accompanied by the sounds of crashing metal.

Thoughts may also intrude more indirectly. The individual may become a bit more vigilant, particularly in matters related to the trauma. Individuals who survive killer tornadoes that devastate their community may become more attentive to weather forecasts and to any darkening that clouds may cause during the day. Some survivors of the Buffalo Creek, West Virginia, flood of 1972 report paying close attention to water levels in the creek whenever it rains (Church, 1974).

Another way in which thoughts may be affected is how individuals think about themselves—their self-esteem (Kilpatrick, Veronen, &

Best, 1985; McCann, Sakheim, & Abrahamson, 1988). Being exposed to highly negative events may decrease self-esteem, at least in the first days or weeks after the trauma. For example, an individual who had many important possessions stolen from her office began to feel "stupid" because, in her words, "I just *cannot* believe I was so stupid as to leave everything there with the door unlocked."

Perhaps the most significant way in which thoughts are affected is the struggle to achieve an understanding of what has occurred (Hodgkinson & Stewart, 1991; Wertheimer, 1991). Trauma survivors ask themselves: "How did this happen?" and "What was the reason for or purpose of this tragedy?" Whether or not the crisis represents a negative psychological event depends in part on the survivor's satisfaction with how he or she addresses and answers these questions. For many people, however, the struggle to understand why bad things have happened is a painful and difficult journey that may never be completely finished.

Emotional Effects

What emotions prevail in people who have been exposed to major stressful events? The specific kinds of emotions that predominate will vary among individuals and across specific circumstances.

One emotion that many individuals experience is *guilt* (Raphael, 1986; Van der Wal, 1990). For example, the mother of a woman who was killed by her estranged husband reviewed in her mind for months the various actions she might have taken to protect her daughter. There is a painful feeling of remorse about what was done or what was left undone or unsaid. This may reflect a belief that certain actions may have prevented the event or that certain actions would have made the loss more bearable. In situations where others suffered much more, the individual may experience the "survivor guilt" seen in people who survived circumstances in which others perished or lost everything they had.

Anger and irritability are often felt by individuals dealing with major life problems (Adler, 1943; McCann et al., 1988). The anger may be expressed at various targets and the irritability may come and go. As an example, the wife of a man who was terminally ill and whose death was imminent became infuriated by what she perceived as the "poor care" her husband was receiving (the care was, in fact, quite good) because she arrived at his hospital bedside one morning and discovered that there was no nurse sitting beside him at the precise moment she opened the door to his room. Other people may simply feel that they are in a "bad mood" much of the time, snapping at others and experiencing brief outbursts of anger. The anger experienced often may be morally justifiable, such as the anger felt by a survivor of sexual assault toward her assailant. Whether specific or diffuse, morally justifiable or not, many individuals who undergo major life stress will experience significant anger.

Perhaps one of the most frequently encountered emotional responses following major life trauma is *fear and anxiety* (Adler, 1943; McCann et al., 1988; Raphael, 1986). When the circumstances to which individuals are exposed involve significant threat to life, health, or to important property, it is likely that those individuals will feel apprehension, worry, and concern for some time following the event. Rape victims, for example, may feel particularly distressed when specific locations or environmental conditions remind them of the assault they experienced (Calhoun & Atkeson, 1991). General worry can also be triggered by such stressful events as major financial loss (Ganzini, McFarland, & Cutler, 1990). Bereaved parents, for example, may worry about the well-being of their surviving children. Whatever the nature of the event, however, anxiety is one of the emotional responses most frequently reported by people who are faced with difficult circumstances in life.

Another general emotional state that is quite common in people dealing with difficult life circumstances is *depression*. Although anxiety is more likely to occur when the trauma involves major threat, depression is more likely when the circumstances involve significant loss. Most mental health professionals (Bowlby, 1980) and laypersons (Quarantelli, 1985) expect people who have experienced significant loss to be depressed. Perhaps because depression *is* so common in people dealing with such events as a death in the family, its absence is sometimes regarded as a sign of mental disorder. Although this view may well be incorrect (Wortman & Silver, 1989), the data do suggest that depression is a common emotional response when major losses are experienced (Calhoun & Atkeson, 1991; Hodgkinson & Stewart, 1991; Raphael, 1986; Rudestam, 1977).

Individuals exposed to highly stressful events are very likely to experience a constellation of distressing emotions. Although the specific patterns will vary from person to person, it is correct to say that unpleasant emotional states are almost certain to occur. In addition to the occurrence of these emotions, some changes in actions and behavior may also occur.

Negative Changes in Behavior

Our society relies on drugs in a variety of ways. Alcohol, tobacco, caffeine, and psychotropic medications are in common use. When individuals confront very difficult events, the use of both legal and illegal drugs can increase (Adams & Adams, 1984; McCann & Pearlman, 1990). Increased drug use is likely when the difficulties created by traumas are long-lived. Survivors may use both prescription and nonprescription drugs, such as alcohol, to help them cope with the psychological distress and pain they are experiencing. Although such increased drug use is not necessarily negative, this is a change in behavior that can add to the individual's difficulties as time passes.

Other changes in behavior may be seen in the individual's withdrawal from others (Schnaier, 1986). Individuals experiencing significant amounts of distressing emotion from traumatic events may believe that others cannot understand them or help them in any significant way (Tedeschi & Calhoun, 1993). The result is that the individual experiencing the crisis may withdraw from others. Individuals who are experiencing distress, particularly emotional responses like depression, may be very difficult people to be around (Coyne & Downey, 1991), so their distress also may take a toll by causing others to avoid them to some degree.

When a survivor's emotional response includes a significant degree of depression, or when the traumatic event itself involves sexual violence (e.g., sexual assault), then sexual difficulties are more likely to occur (Calhoun & Atkeson, 1991; Wilkinson, 1983). The person may experience not only a decreased interest in sex, but also sexual dysfunction. For example, women may experience difficulty in achieving orgasm and men may experience erectile difficulties.

A final negative impact of traumatic events on behavior is a possible increase in aggressive behavior. For some, this may occur when there has also been an increase in alcohol use (Schnaier, 1986). A particularly pernicious impact of traumatic events may occur when the events involve the physical or sexual abuse of children (Greven, 1990; Kendall-Tackett, Williams, & Finkelhor, 1993; Malinovsky-Rummell & Hansen, 1993; McCann et al., 1988). Not only will the abuse of a child produce many of the negative consequences described already, but such aggressive treatment of children may lead some of them to become aggressive as adults.

In summary, traumatic circumstances can have negative effects on our thoughts by invading consciousness, affecting dreams, increasing vigilance, lowering self-esteem, and creating a struggle to understand what has happened. Traumatic events can create distressing emotions that include feelings of guilt, anger, fear, and depression. Traumatic events can also produce negative changes in behavior, including increased use of drugs, difficulties with sexual desire and performance, withdrawal from others, and, in some circumstances, increased aggressive behavior. These events can also have physical consequences.

PHYSICAL PROBLEMS AND COMPLAINTS

Most people will be able to recall a particular event where "the adrenaline was flowing" in their own bodies. The various systems of the body that are activated when the adrenaline flows prepare the body for fighting or running away. The various systems of the body are aroused so that maximum energy can be used. This extreme arousal of the bodily systems is evidenced by increased heart rate, more rapid breathing, muscle tension, dry mouth, elevated blood pressure, and general readiness to respond to the environment (i.e., sympathetic nervous system response) (Selye, 1950). Individuals exposed to highly traumatic events that occur unexpectedly will experience this increase in arousal. For many, this increase in activation of the body will not readily subside, and it is one of the most common complaints associated with highly stressful events (Hodgkinson & Stewart, 1991; Wilson, 1989). Events that remind the person of the trauma may produce this unwanted response of the autonomic nervous system. For example, a fighter pilot experienced hyperarousal when he attempted to return to his pastime of hunting after returning home from war.

Because of the chronic arousability of the bodily systems, it is not surprising that people dealing with highly stressful events also report experiencing fatigue (Wilkinson, 1983). A long list of other common physical complaints has also been found in the aftermath of major life crises. These complaints include gastrointestinal difficulties, headaches, loss of appetite, difficulty breathing freely, a variety of aches and pains, and urinary problems. There does not appear to be a specific physical syndrome produced by traumatic events, but it is clear that the experience of physical discomfort is common in people who are dealing with traumatic events and that the specific discomfort takes different forms.

Much of the initial study of the impact of life stress was focused on the link between life stress and physical illness. Although much of the early research was hampered by methodological limitations, the conclusions of the early work still hold up. There is a link between exposure to significant stress and the development of physical illness, and there is evidence that immune functioning is compromised by stress (Kaplan, 1991; Kiecolt-Glaser & Glaser, 1989; O'Leary, 1990). But several important qualifications must be made. The occurrence of disease depends on many factors, some of which are more important than the presence or absence of stress. In addition, the individual's risk of disease will be moderated by many other factors, such as the person's general health before exposure to stress, the quality of the stress management practices the individual uses (e.g., exercise, proper nutrition), and the availability of support from friends and family (Kamarck, Manuck, & Jennings, 1990; Kobasa, 1979). Overall, however, exposure to traumatic events does moderately increase the likelihood that physical disease will occur (Herbert & Cohen, 1993).

LIFE STRESS AND PSYCHIATRIC DISORDER

Exposure to highly stressful circumstances leads to significant psychological and physical distress. But does exposure to trauma increase the individual's chances of developing psychiatric disorders? The available data suggest that exposure to stressful events puts a person at increased risk for the development of such disorders (Garbarino, Kostelny, & Durow, 1991; Rubonis & Bickman, 1991). However, it is very important to keep in mind that most people who are exposed to high levels of stress will *not* develop psychiatric disorders. Although group comparisons clearly indicate that exposure to traumatic events does produce a general increase in the risk of psychiatric impairment, there are many factors that can reduce or even eliminate that risk altogether. For example, individuals who have successfully coped with life in the past and who have strong, loving relationships with other people are much less likely to develop psychological disorders following exposure to trauma than people without these experiences.

For those who do develop psychiatric difficulties following exposure to severe stress, the most likely impairments involve anxiety disorders or clinical depression (Ganzini et al., 1990; Shore, Tatum, & Vollmer, 1986). Psychiatric impairment involving anxiety includes phobias, posttraumatic stress disorder, generalized anxiety, and panic attacks. Depressive problems include sad mood, loss of interest and pleasure in life, low levels of self-esteem, low energy level, problems sleeping, and other similar complaints. Although these kinds of difficulties are the most commonly associated with exposure to high levels of stress, any of the psychological difficulties recognized as disorders may in part be precipitated by exposure to such stress. For individuals experiencing extreme amounts of life trauma, the stressful event may precipitate a specific constellation of psychological symptoms, such as a dissociative disorder (e.g., amnesia, multiple personality or dissociative identity disorder) or a posttraumatic stress disorder (American Psychiatric Association, 1994).

A general reminder is in order. The group rate of psychiatric impairment goes up for people who undergo high levels of life stress. But there are many factors that contribute to the development of psychiatric problems (e.g., genetics, biological disorders), and exposure to traumatic events is only one of many such contributory factors.

Does Time Heal All Wounds?

The typical person who undergoes a significant trauma in life will experience psychological and physical distress in a variety of ways, and the likelihood of psychiatric disorder and physical illness also can increase. In the event that high levels of distress are experienced, won't time be the best healer of all?

Some people who are exposed to demanding life situations will not show any of the forms of distress we have cataloged (Quarantelli, 1985; Wortman & Silver, 1989). These people may not show obvious signs of distress, and they will not be overwhelmed emotionally by the events they must face. For example, on the day after her husband was killed in a tornado, one woman was back at work. She did not show any signs of severe emotional distress, and when asked about that, she indicated that she would miss her husband, but that "life just has to go on."

Traditional psychological approaches have suggested that such people are denying their pain, pushing it out of their awareness. The traditional expectation is that such repression or denial will produce a lack of apparent distress now, but the repressed emotions will cause psychological problems for the individual in the future. Although it is possible that some people are coping by using psychological defenses to keep distress out of their awareness, it is also likely that some individuals are capable of coping successfully with overwhelmingly difficult demands without experiencing either the distress or the impairment that is typical for most people facing similar challenges. For some people, then, time is not necessary to heal wounds because there are no wounds to heal—there are simply difficult situations that have been successfully handled.

However, most people will experience some form of distress as they cope with highly demanding life situations. We have summarized some of the most typical above. Will time be a healer for these people? For most of them, yes. Within about 2 years of a major trauma, most people dealing with most difficulties have returned to the level of psychological functioning they had prior to the traumatic episode (Calhoun & Atkeson, 1991). However, this is a generalization that must be made with caution because it addresses the "typical" person. For most individuals who have had to confront major traumatic events in their lives, over time there will be an elimination of most of the distress generated by the tragedies they have faced. It is important to recognize that *time itself* is not the healer. What produces healing are certain experiences and coping mechanisms used during this period of dealing with the aftermath of the trauma. For example, the traumatic events may be reviewed in a victim's mind dozens of times before the reality of the trauma is accepted and a sense of guilt is relieved.

The sad truth is that for some people, time may not be a healer at all (Lehman, Wortman, & Williams, 1987). The psychological distress precipitated by the traumatic event may persist for a long time, perhaps for the rest of their lives. Although clinicians and therapists often speak of the need for individuals dealing with crisis to reach a state of "resolution" about their experiences, this may not be possible for some people. Those who never successfully come to terms with their difficulties are probably a minority, but their long-lasting pain is an unavoidable truth that both professionals and laypersons must acknowledge. For some people, the pain will clearly never subside.

Is There a Positive Side?

In this chapter, we have summarized the available literature on the negative aspects of life trauma. The knowledge available seems to justify the pessimistic stance that researchers, clinicians, and laypersons have about the psychological consequences of traumatic events. In the words of Charles Dickens, the available information tells us that traumas in life may lead to "the worst of times." This is a truth we cannot negate. Facing natural catastrophes, major losses, the death of someone we love, unexpected and prolonged unemployment, divorce, and any other trauma will painfully test our ability to cope.

Although such traumas can lead to the worst of times, struggling with the crises in our lives can also lead to the best of times by providing us with the opportunity for psychological growth that would not be possible without the challenge of the traumatic event. It is the very act of struggling with the many negative consequences of traumatic events that makes possible the varied forms of psychological growth on which we will focus in the next chapter.

PSYCHOLOGICAL GROWTH FROM TRAUMA

Research Findings

So much pain has to have happened for a reason.
—Salvadoran political prisoner

In Chapter 1, we saw how theologians, philosophers, and writers have recognized and described the possibility for personal growth in life traumas. We also saw how some have seen existential wisdom as dependent on the experience of these challenges, the struggle to live through them, and the changes they demand. As we reported in Chapter 2, researchers have studied extensively the negative effects of traumas as opposed to the positive impact of these events. But there has been an anecdotal and theoretical recognition of the positive effects of trauma (Caplan, 1964; Lipowski, 1970; V. Taylor, 1977), and then more solid data on this phenomenon (Hamera & Shontz, 1978; Houston, Bloom, Burish, & Cummings, 1978; Wilson & Spencer, 1990). Recently, there have been attempts to account for this psychological growth (Hager, 1992; Nerken, 1993; Schaefer & Moos, 1992) by using contemporary theories as explanations for the process of developing profound and healthy insights into living as a result of surviving trauma.

In this chapter, we will review the benefits that people living beyond traumas often perceive. Although there are only a few studies that have provided direct information on the kinds of perceived benefits reported by respondents, there are consistencies in the available data. Schaefer and Moos (1992) suggested a categorization scheme for these changes that included improved coping skills, "social resources," and "personal resources." We have organized this growth somewhat differently into categories of changes in self-perception, interpersonal relationships, and philosophy of life.

Perceived Changes in Self:
Self-Reliance and Vulnerability

One class of benefits cited by individuals who have faced difficult experiences is positive changes in perception of the self. Affleck and colleagues (Affleck, Allen, Tennen, McGrade, & Ratzan, 1985; Affleck, Tennen, & Gershman, 1985) reported in two studies that respondents indicated that "emotional growth" was a positive outcome of dealing with their difficulties. Andreasen and Norris (1972) indicated that some burn patients reported that the reason they had experienced their trauma was to make them better people. People dealing with bereavement have reported a variety of positive changes resulting from their struggle with grief (Calhoun & Tedeschi, 1989-1990; Hamera & Shontz, 1978; Lehman et al., 1993; Lopata, 1973). Eighty-three percent of a sample of people who survived the sinking of a cruise ship reported that they felt more experienced about life (Joseph, Williams, & Yule, 1993). Collins, Taylor, and Skokan (1990) stated that the most common positive change in self reported in a sample of cancer patients was feeling stronger and more self-assured. Similar findings have been reported for some people dealing with divorce (Schlesinger, 1982; Wallerstein, 1986), combat experience (Aldwin, Levenson, & Spiro, 1994; Elder & Clipp, 1989), captivity during time of war (Sledge, Boydstun, & Rabe, 1980), and bone marrow transplantation (Curbow, Somerfield, Baker, Wingard, & Legro, 1993).

INCREASED SELF-RELIANCE AND PERSONAL STRENGTH

Living through life traumas provides a great deal of information about self-reliance. These experiences affect not only the perceptions of competence in various situations but the likelihood that one will choose to address difficulties in an assertive fashion. To the degree that traumatic events produce coping responses that are initially unsuccessful, self-reliance may be questioned. Continuing failure to resolve the problem may eventually produce the judgment that one is incapable of producing desired outcomes, and essentially helpless in the face of it all. But concomitant factors may help to produce people who are able to experience a perception of increased self-reliance as a result of coping with trauma. One factor is the availability of others who are good models of coping.

In one of our studies (Tedeschi & Calhoun, 1988), we found that people who had become physically disabled often referred to others with similar problems who demonstrated how to cope. These demonstrations may involve specific behaviors that enable survivors of trauma to make their situation more bearable. For example, one study participant told of observing the remarkable wheelchair-handling technique of a fellow rehabilitation patient and determining to adopt this daring and aggressive style of getting around in the chair. This new ability allowed him to experience more pride and a sense of self-reliance because he found that he was able to do things with the chair that his therapists and other patients tended to discourage. It appears that people who have similar problems are often the most credible sources of information.

Some traumatic events appear to limit the possibilities for people, as in the case of physical disabilities. For people confronting this type of trauma, finding enhanced self-reliance depends on a focus on the ways of handling this difficulty with personal creativity and fortitude. But other life traumas may open up new possibilities where self-reliance can be achieved. Studies of bereaved elderly women (Calhoun & Tedeschi, 1989-1990; Lund, Caserta, & Dimond, 1993) found that many women who had filled a very traditional role of wife in the family discovered latent abilities to handle many things that their husbands had reserved within their masculine roles. These women recounted stories of learning how to manage financial matters, dealing with business and service people, and even working for the first time.

A psychotherapy client of one of the authors described a similar circumstance. This woman had suffered apparently hypochondriacal symptoms and had been bedridden and hospitalized on many occasions with no apparent improvement. Family therapy produced some good effects, but the greatest changes in this woman's outlook and behavior occurred some years later after her husband became disabled. She became a caretaker for him and learned to do many things for which he had previously been responsible. She proudly declared that she had even learned to tune up the car!

People coping with a traumatic event often draw the conclusion that they are stronger as a result (Thomas, DiGiulio, & Sheehan, 1991). If they are able to cope successfully with such rough times, they can cope with anything (Calhoun & Tedeschi, 1989-1990); that is, their self-reliance is substantially elevated beyond what it was before the trauma as a result of meeting the most difficult challenge they have faced. This seems to be experienced as a feeling of strength and confidence that generalizes to all kinds of situations less difficult than the trauma that has been faced.

There is a vast literature in psychology that links perceptions of control over events to a sense of well-being (Langer & Rodin, 1976; Schultz, 1980; Wallston & Wallston, 1982), although this relationship is not simple and clear-cut (Burger, 1989; Folkman, 1984; Thompson, 1981). It appears that the most psychologically healthy people maintain a sense of personal control beyond what could be supported factually (Taylor & Brown, 1988). Therefore, any outcomes that bolster this sense of self-reliance can be seen as contributions to psychological well-being, both perceived and demonstrated in behavior. This may occur even if the initial event was not handled successfully, or if survival may have been due to chance. Many Holocaust survivors, for example, see themselves as lucky to have survived, yet have shown a remarkable tendency to be assertive and tenacious in their postwar lives (Helmreich, 1992).

Many people may be more successful in coping with the consequences of trauma because the chronic experience of these consequences can be thoughtfully considered, whereas the initial traumas catch people off guard. Continuing life difficulties can present another opportunity for personal success. For example, a firefighter who had saved lives over the years felt a great deal of guilt after having been unable to save the life of his own child after a tree fell on him in a freak accident in a neighbor's yard. Initially, he found himself unable to return to work because of the anxiety he felt whenever an emergency call came. He recognized that the trauma of his child's death was more difficult than any traumatic event he had faced before, despite his professional training. He eventually came to appreciate the strength he found in himself to overcome his guilt and grief, and finally saw himself as a more effective firefighter than he had ever been. His own loss sensitized him to the importance of his work and the responsibility he had for the lives of others, and children in particular. This recognition, and his return to work, were victories that helped offset his sense of failure at his inability to save his child.

There is certainly no expectation on the part of survivors of traumas that anything good will come from these events. But the psychological approaches that may be learned from others, as well as new behaviors that are practiced, can ultimately lead to a recognition that an important new sense of self-reliance was gained through the struggle.

RECOGNITION AND APPRECIATION OF VULNERABILITY

Surviving trauma may also lead to an enhanced appreciation of one's vulnerability, sensitivity, and emotional experience. At first glance, a recognition that one is vulnerable may not appear to be a positive outcome of trauma, but among people who have illusions of invulnerability, to the extent that they were functioning in dangerous and unhealthy ways physically and psychologically, a change in this regard can be seen as positive, even by the person who undergoes this change. In the case of Jerry, the paralyzed man with whose statement we began Chapter 1, the accident that produced his paralysis also produced a recognition that his lifestyle would have eventually killed him. For him, his paralysis was a small price to pay for this knowledge. Jerry believed that only this "ton of bricks" could have convinced him that his lifestyle was dangerous for him and that he was indeed vulnerable. He described his unseen vulnerabilities as physical; that is, his drug use would eventually catch up with him. He also saw himself as vulnerable psychologically in that he had alienated himself from his family and was suffering as a result of this separation. The camaraderie of his rock band and his drug abuse had dulled the recognition of this fact. He also came to see himself as spiritually vulnerable in that he neglected his spiritual life and viewed it as irrelevant given his assumed physical invulnerability.

Because a sense of invulnerability is associated particularly with the male gender role, a change in this excessive sense of unassailable strength is another positive change in the perception of self that occurs in the struggle with trauma (Tedeschi, 1989). A loss or a tragedy challenges this sense of invulnerability, as does the recognition that it may be impossible to cope with it without some assistance. Of course, as long as one maintains the belief that one is invulnerable, asking for help has little salience. But the extremes of trauma create totally new conditions, and men who could afford to be at the extremes of self-reliance can now find themselves submitting to the recognition that what has happened is too much for them to bear alone.

We have discussed the phenomenon in which coping with a life crisis can lead to the perceptions of oneself as more capable and self-reliant, yet crises can also make clear that one is vulnerable. Can the sense of both vulnerability and self-reliance develop in tandem? It appears that this does indeed happen and that the parallel developments of self-reliance and vulnerability, as reflected in the use of available help in the social support network, are complementary. It has become apparent that the ability to use a variety of coping responses is related to good outcomes and the perception of benefits in coping with trauma (Collins et al., 1990). This is recognized in military training. A series of small crises is arranged to break down the sense of invulnerability and to demonstrate the need to function within a unit of other people on whom one relies. At the same time, a sense of an ability to handle these crises is enhanced with the experience of success during the training exercises.

A Changed Sense
of Relationship With Others

From the foregoing discussion of the effects of changes in the sense of one's ability to rely on oneself and in the degree to which one is vulnerable, it is clear that important positive changes in relationships with others can be expected. For example, Affleck, Tennen, and Gershman (1985) described reactions of mothers of newborns to the experience of having their babies treated for severe perinatal medical problems in a neonatal intensive care unit. Almost 60% of the mothers in this sample reported some perceived benefits, with 20% mentioning benefits involving closer family relationships, emotional growth, and an appreciation of how precious their child is. Similar reactions were found in a group of adults who had lost a parent within the preceding 2 years (Malinak, Hoyt, & Patterson, 1979; Zemore & Shepel, 1989). Approximately half of these people reported a deepening of their relationships with others as they realized how important these relationships were, and how quickly they could be lost (see also Affleck, Allen, Tennen, McGrade, & Ratzan, 1985). Not all people experiencing the loss of a loved one report improved relationships, but at least a minority do (Lehman, Lang, Wortman, & Sorenson, 1989; Lehman et al., 1993). The improvement in relationships following traumatic events may occur more often with some types of relationships, such as with family members, than with others (Drabek & Key, 1976).

SELF-DISCLOSURE AND EMOTIONAL EXPRESSIVENESS

The results of a study with a sample of bereaved, predominantly elderly women (Calhoun & Tedeschi, 1989-1990) demonstrate how these improved relationships came about. Eighty-three percent of these people reported that they realized through their bereavement that they had family and friends on whom they could depend, and 60% found themselves expressing emotion in a more open way. This may indicate that a combination of the positive responses of others, and the openness to assistance of those in need, may be related to the recognition of the availability and importance of strong interpersonal relationships.

When people are confronted with traumatic events, the continuing need for discussion of the consequences of these events and the need to cope can lead them to become more self-disclosing. Although the reactions of people in the support network may vary (Dakof & Taylor, 1990), in general, experiences of self-disclosure provide an opportunity to try out these new behaviors, which then can be directed at the most appropriate people in the support network. The recognition of one's vulnerability can lead, especially in men, to more emotional expressiveness, willingness to accept help, and therefore an employment of social supports that had previously been ignored.

For example, a successful executive was 50 years old when he became unemployed for the first time in his life. This unemployment stretched past a year, and he began to recognize that all kinds of positive things were occurring in the midst of his financial disaster. He had always traveled on business, but now he was home with his wife again, and, as a result, their relationship improved. Part of this improvement was because he expressed his vulnerability in a way that allowed his wife to see him sympathetically for the first time in years. She discovered that she had valuable support to offer him. He was also able to reflect on his management style and consider why the company chose to let him go. He came to see that he was aloof and assumed that he did not need to build bridges to other people within the company. He determined specific ways to manage differently in the future, both to protect his own position and to enhance the working atmosphere of his employees. He even did something he never thought he could do for fear of feeling humiliated: He joined a support group for other unemployed people. He recognized that he was no longer in the special position of being invulnerable. He cultivated a newfound ability to be more emotionally expressive in the support group and at home. He recognized through experiencing his own anxieties and doubts that he was much more like other human beings whom he had previously distanced himself from, if not held in contempt. He valued these changes and regretted that he had not learned how to live this way many years ago.

Another example of how the recognition of vulnerability can lead to more self-disclosure and intimacy in relationships was provided by a young man who was sentenced to life in prison at the age of 18 for stabbing someone during a rampage while he was under the influence of drugs. He reported that since his incarceration, he had found himself becoming much more open emotionally to his mother and siblings than he had ever been. He recognized that circumstances in his family, especially his father's drinking and severe abuse of the rest of the family, had produced a toughness and alienation in him. As a result, he found himself unable to ask for help. Now he came to see that he was in need of help, open to addressing the issues in the family, and more hopeful about his life than he had ever been before.

COMPASSION, EMPATHY, AND EFFORT IN RELATIONSHIPS

Part of the positive development of social relationships among survivors comes from their increased compassion, greater sensitivity to the needs and feelings of other people, and efforts directed at improving relationships (Collins et al., 1990; Miles, Demi, & Mostyn-Aker, 1984). As a result, people who suffer from trauma may be more likely to offer support to others in turn (Tedeschi, 1989; Wuthnow, 1991). For example, many bereaved parents report that because of their grief, they are more cognizant of the deaths of children and more concerned for the children's parents. They notice obituaries and other news of these deaths. They find themselves sending notes and making phone calls to strangers with whom they now relate as a result of their shared grief. Although some people might judge this to be indicative of a preoccupation with death and an overidentification with others, bereaved parents' experiences of relating to others in this way often promotes a sense of having completed a substantial portion of the healing process. If one is ready and able to help others, this must indicate that one is reasonably healthy.

Another aspect of improving relationships after traumatic events was reported by Veronen and Kilpatrick (1983) in a study of rape survivors. The women who came for counseling learned to discriminate positive from negative relationships. This changed approach to relationships allowed them to become better able to establish more positive and intimate relationships with family members from whom they had been estranged.

A Changed Philosophy of Life

Change in one's philosophy of life is another benefit reported by many people coping with life traumas. For example, Malinak et al. (1979) found that some of their bereaved respondents reported an increased appreciation for their own existence, and Affleck, Tennen, and Gershman (1985) noted in their study that an improved perspective on life was reported by 23% of the mothers of sick newborns. Taylor, Lichtman, and Wood (1984) reported that of women who had made changes since their cancer was discovered, 60% described positive changes in priorities, such as taking life easier and enjoying it more. A strong sense of reordered priorities has also been reported by bereaved parents (Klass, 1986-1987). Ninety-four percent of the survivors of the cruise ship *Jupiter* stated that they no longer took life for granted and 71% reported that they now lived each day to the fullest (Joseph et al., 1993). Survivors who experience extreme stress, illness, and the death of loved ones lose their sense of invulnerability. They confront the inevitability of death. As a result, they gain a new appreciation for life. Some people recognize as never before that their time and their relationships are precious. They acquire a renewed appreciation for simple moments in everyday life and the relationships formerly taken for granted (Miles & Crandall, 1983). Lagrande (1988) quotes a young woman who lost her mother and brother and who illustrates this philosophy: " 'If you love someone, let them know it now. They might not be here tomorrow' " (p. 161).

The changed philosophy of life may have a spiritual component (Calhoun & Tedeschi, 1989-1990; Miles et al., 1984; Pargament et al., 1990). For some people, major trauma can precipitate a spiritual search that may not be concluded satisfactorily. Such people, for example, may become more cynical and less religious (Schwartzberg & Janoff-Bulman, 1991). However, for a significant number of individuals confronted with significant life challenges, the ensuing struggle may lead to a strengthening of religious beliefs (Andrykowski, 1992; Calhoun & Tedeschi, 1989-1990; Calhoun, Tedeschi, & Lincourt, 1992; Schwartzberg & Janoff-Bulman, 1991). Although for some, spiritual beliefs may be temporarily weakened by tragedy, the struggle to understand the negative event can lead eventually to strengthened beliefs.

A woman whose fiancé died in an automobile accident described her experience this way: "My beliefs are strengthened now, but I did go dead for awhile. At first I doubted everything, but now my faith is even stronger than it was before. I pray more." Pargament et al. (1990) point out that a strengthening of religious beliefs may serve a variety of purposes for an individual coping with trauma, and that these purposes vary among individuals. These purposes include *gaining a sense of control* over a life that has become uncontrollable. Placing one's decisions "in the hands of God" represents a paradox of gaining this control by giving it up. This may also bring *comfort*, especially when the person is struggling with difficult decisions in the aftermath of trauma. Pargament et al. (1990) also describe the personal *intimacy* that some people feel with God when this relationship seems strong and personal. This can offset the loneliness and isolation that the victimization or its aftermath may produce. Finally, *meaning* can be found in religious concepts about life and suffering, as we saw in Chapter 1. Recognizing meaning in the midst of trauma and its aftermath allows a person to experience emotional relief because the questioning, searching, and despair tend to maintain strong negative emotions. Perceiving meaning can allow the development of a new philosophy of life that alters the most basic assumptions that people hold about how life works and what meaning it may have (Janoff-Bulman, 1989a; Taylor & Brown, 1988; Thompson & Janigian, 1988).

The effects of traumatic life events on this overarching view of one's life may be profound. The narrative or storyline of one's life is generated from a variety of incidents or scenes as well as idealized images of the self (McAdams, 1989). People confronted with these events must come to terms with how their attempts to cope reflect their narrative, which they have been creating for themselves, or how their coping has interrupted the assumed storyline. It appears that benefits are derived from such experiences to the extent that these life scenes are incorporated as dramatic devices or plot twists that further the narrative.

For example, many participants in our study of coping with physical handicaps (Tedeschi & Calhoun, 1988) described their injuries and subsequent attempts to cope as a "reckoning time" or a "crossroads" in life. Their lives were forever changed but deepened by the apparently unfortunate events. The deepening inevitably had to do with the issues of relating to others in a more positive way and learning about one's own vulnerability, power, and self-reliance. They incorporated these qualities into their lives by savoring their experiences with others and taking on new, personally meaningful challenges.

One young person who was paralyzed decided to go to college, and he claimed that he had formed better friendships than ever before. He thought that his wheelchair put him in a position in which he sometimes had to ask for help. As a result, he found his chair to be a conversation piece that enabled him to make contacts with others, which he nurtured into friendships. He also came to feel that there was no reason for him to delay certain adventures he'd always dreamed of, so he took a trip around Europe, alone in his wheelchair. These acts gave him a clear sense that his life path had shifted dramatically. The crossroads could have led him to despair and immobilization, yet he struck out on the opposite path. In doing so, he created a narrative in which his injury became a positive event. He now understands his life and lives it in a much more meaningful way. This may be what is often meant by finding meaning in these events (Epstein, 1990; Frankl, 1963; Tait & Silver, 1989).

This process of assimilating the trauma into the life narrative and into the fundamental assumptions about life, or changing the narrative and assumptions to accommodate what has happened, involves great effort (Epstein, 1990; Janoff-Bulman & Timko, 1987; Tait & Silver, 1989; Tennen & Affleck, 1990). But despite these efforts and the profound changes that may be wrought in the survivors' fundamental understanding of life and its proper path, outcomes are perceived by the survivors as beneficial. The benefits come from the newfound order and purpose that this meaning provides (Thompson & Janigian, 1988), not only to the event itself but also to other aspects of life with which it must relate to become integrated into the life narrative. This can produce a subjective sense that life has improved in a fundamental way despite the unfortunate event. This may be due to the relationship between self-perceptions of control and esteem, and psychological well-being or happiness, no matter what the objective life circumstances may be (Campbell, 1981; Diener, 1984).

When one can firmly grasp meaning and see one's life as orderly and purposeful, perceptions of control and esteem are likely to follow, and with these, a sense of well-being. From this introduction to this kind of perceived benefit, it may be easier to understand Jerry's statement quoted at the beginning of this book about the accident that paralyzed him: "If I had it to do all over again, . . . I would not want it not to happen."

Conclusions

At least three groups of benefits have been reported in studies of responses to critical life problems. First, we discussed changes in the perceived self as well as the behaviors related to this self. A greater perceived self-reliance and a greater recognition of one's vulnerability were associated with a variety of new behaviors that allows more successful coping. Modeling of these behaviors and ways to understand the changes in one's status resulting from the trauma are provided by those in the social support network, especially those who have had some experience with a similar situation. The ability to use these social supports arises from the recognition of vulnerability that the trauma makes clear. This perceived vulnerability allows a person to place him- or herself within relationships with others in a way that allows them to be accessible to help. As a result, a second important benefit is realized: a healthier connection with other people. This may allow changes in the overall perspective on life's meaning and appropriate priorities. This is the third major benefit that appears to accrue from the struggle with traumatic life events.

Associated with this may be changes in basic assumptions about how and why the events in life occur (Collins et al., 1990; Janoff-Bulman & Timko, 1987), spiritual beliefs, and what should be done to address the purpose in life that is now clarified. Although the events may be tragic, people can come to value the struggle with them. Some people, such as Holocaust survivors and bereaved parents, always perceive the trauma they survived as negative (Whiteman, 1993), although they can perceive some benefits in the struggle with the event and its aftermath. Other people no longer perceive themselves as having been victimized by the traumatic events, and may in some way value these events. But all who experience personal growth as a result of trauma strengthened themselves by struggling merely to cope at the start, then made discoveries experienced as profoundly enlightening, and then incorporated these discoveries into a life path viewed with satisfaction and pride.

PERSONALITY CHARACTERISTICS AND SUCCESSFUL COPING

Character cannot be developed in ease and quiet. Only through experience of trial and suffering can the soul be strengthened, vision cleared, ambition inspired, and success achieved.

—Helen Keller

People who are successful at coping with negative events have carried a variety of labels in the psychological literature. In this chapter, we will summarize these related conceptualizations and link the common elements of these personality types. It will become clear that people tend to appraise negative events in characteristic ways and engage in certain behavioral strategies. In succeeding chapters, we will discuss the appraisal and behavioral coping processes after painting a general picture of those who are successful at coping, thereby setting the stage for survivors' perceptions of growth in this process.

Positive outcomes in life traumas depend on the coming together of several elements. One element is an event perceived as a formidable challenge. A second element is personality characterized by persistence, determination, confidence, an ability to make emotional connections with others, and acceptance of the limitations of circumstances when necessary. Bandura (1982b) points out that chance occurrences provide an opportunity for a change in life paths, but that these opportunities produce a change only if a person has an available set of skills to take advantage of them. A combination of flexibility and tenacity appears to produce benefits. This type of personality has elements of internal locus of control (Rotter, 1966); self-efficacy (Bandura, 1977, 1982a) or self-confidence (Schaefer & Moos, 1992); optimism (Scheier & Carver, 1985); hardiness (Kobasa, 1979); resilience (Beardslee & Podorefsky, 1988; Green, 1986; Rutter, 1987; Werner, 1984); sense of coherence (Antonovsky, 1987); and creativity (Strickland, 1989). These overlapping characteristics can promote a willingness to approach the process of overcoming and benefiting from crisis, as described previously, with the proper respect for what cannot be changed and the persistence to work toward difficult changes that remain possible. We will discuss the characteristics of people who cope well with trauma and some research that indicates that they may be particularly adept at finding benefits in these events. In the final section of this chapter, we will consider how personality characteristics fit together to create a person who is well equipped to cope successfully. We will also discuss the benefits of this coping process for survivors.

Locus of Control

Much of our understanding of the personal characteristics that allow people to perceive benefits in crises comes from social learning theory. Almost all of the characteristics discussed below originate in the locus of control construct devised by Rotter (1966). This construct refers to people's perceptions and beliefs that what they do is or is not related to events that follow. People with an internal locus of control tend to see themselves as affecting outcomes of events, whereas those with an external locus of control attribute events to the actions of other people, chance, or fate. Rotter conceptualized locus of control as a "generalized expectancy," a set of predictions made across situations that is especially powerful when a specific situation is novel.

In early research on locus of control, it was found that an internal locus of control predicted resistance to influence from others (Crowne & Liverant, 1963), seeking information about one's health status, being more assertive about medical care (Seeman & Evans, 1962), and willingness to take decisive actions for social change (Gore & Rotter, 1963). To the degree that a life crisis is novel and there is ambiguity about how much control an individual has over producing certain outcomes to the crisis, generalized expectancies for locus of control of reinforcement can become important in determining whether people will act in ways to use the control they expect to have, or allow others to make decisions or let events take their course without attempting to alter them. Aversive situations produce attempts to reassert control (Thompson, 1981), and such efforts can lead to more effective coping behavior and a sense of meaning and coherence. As Strickland (1989) has pointed out, an external locus of control is related to Seligman's (1975) concept of "learned helplessness," which occurs when people (or animals) perceive no relationship between their actions and aversive events, leading to the belief that there is no means of escape from what is distressing or threatening. However, individuals who have extreme beliefs in their own ability to control outcomes may find traumatic events significantly more difficult to cope with than people with more moderate assumptions of personal control (Perloff, 1983; Swindle, Heller, & Lakey, 1988). Although people with extreme beliefs that they cannot control outcomes may underestimate how they could find ways to solve problems, people with extreme beliefs in their abilities to control might unrealistically believe that they can influence existential aspects of problems (Fisher & Fisher, 1993).

Self-Efficacy

Bandura (1982a) has described self-efficacy as a perception that one can successfully perform certain behaviors required to deal with prospective situations. This perception influences judgments that people make about what they will try to do. People avoid actions that they believe will exceed their capabilities, whereas a strong sense of self-efficacy will lead them to exert greater effort to master challenges. This makes the likelihood of success greater. Success in turn promotes self-efficacy, although there are other routes to enhanced self-efficacy, including seeing others act successfully (vicarious experiences), others' persuasion, and physiological indicants that convince people they are sufficiently calm and physically able to act successfully.

Bandura's (1986) social learning approach posits that events become threatening when people judge that they cannot be effective in coping with them. Bandura emphasizes that thought-produced arousal plays a large role in generating distress. He makes a distinction between the frightening thoughts and the anxiety that they produce. It is not frightening thoughts by themselves that produce anxiety, but the perception of a lack of self-efficacy in turning off these thoughts (Bandura, 1988). People with a low perceived self-efficacy become preoccupied with inefficacy, magnify threats, and worry about things that are not likely to happen. When people high in perceived self-efficacy believe that their efforts will be fairly rewarded, they tend to engage in what Bandura (1982a) describes as "assured, opportune action" (p. 140). If they do not believe that their actions, which they can perform with skill, will be fairly rewarded, they may protest or try to change their environment. Whether or not rewards are forthcoming, self-efficacy may allow an approach to problems that is more beneficial to the individual than the resignation, apathy, self-devaluation, or despondency that Bandura predicts for those low in perceived self-efficacy.

Relinquishing control leaves one vulnerable, and this is quite different from knowing that one has control and can freely choose whether or not to use it. This available choice produces a sense of being in command (Bandura, 1988). Therefore, doing away with anxiety is not the goal of coping behavior. Instead, a sense of mastery or self-efficacy develops through the use of choices to approach what is threatening or to withdraw when events arouse high levels of anxiety and to return to what is threatening after anxiety decreases. Confidence in one's ability to cope with anxiety and other negative emotions has also been discussed by Wasch and Kirsch (1992) as generalized expectancies for mood regulation. They have found that people who expect that they can successfully regulate their mood are more likely to take action and find something positive about threats.

Optimism

Maintenance of hope across many life situations or the generalized expectancy that good things will happen are definitions of optimism

(Scheier & Carver, 1985; Tiger, 1979; Weinstein, 1980). Although superficially related to locus of control and self-efficacy, optimism focuses directly on how events will turn out (Scheier & Carver, 1992), rather than who controls them or how well one can perform acts that may affect them. However, optimism, like internal locus of control and perceived self-efficacy, is associated with the use of an active, problem-focused style of dealing with stressors, allowing the avoidance of unproductive immersion in feelings of distress that may accompany stress. For example, dispositional optimists have reported being bothered by fewer physical complaints (Scheier & Carver, 1985), and, when undergoing cardiac rehabilitation, had faster recovery rates than pessimists as a result of their active problem-solving style during the rehabilitation effort (Scheier & Carver, 1987; Scheier et al., 1989). Superior outcomes for optimists were attributed to their ability to remain focused on dealing with their problems.

Optimists tend to use coping strategies that are active and problem focused, and they are willing to put other things aside to deal with problems effectively (Carver & Scheier, 1987). Optimism was associated with resignation or acceptance only in circumstances that were seen as uncontrollable (Scheier, Weintraub, & Carver, 1986). This may mean that optimism is an advantage even under uncontrollable circumstances because it is associated with being able to perceive when defeat is inevitable. It may be easier to accept an isolated defeat when being optimistic about events generally. Perhaps most important for our discussion, there is some evidence (Scheier et al., 1986) that optimists emphasize the positive aspects of their difficult situation, allowing them to redirect their attention to appropriate problem-focused coping strategies in situations that are controllable. Optimism may be inversely related to the broader trait of neuroticism, a tendency to have negative emotions, preoccupation, and insecurity. There are several studies that demonstrate a negative association of Scheier and Carver's (1985) measure of optimism, the Life Orientation Test, with measures of neuroticism such as the NEO Personality Inventory Neuroticism scale (Tedeschi, Calhoun, & Gross, 1993), the Taylor Manifest Anxiety Scale, and the State-Trait Anxiety Inventory trait form (Smith, Pope, Rhodewalt, & Poulton, 1989). In addition, other measures of optimism have also been negatively correlated with measures of neuroticism (Darvill & Johnson, 1991; Smith et al., 1989).

Optimists appear to be less anxious, hostile, depressed, self-conscious, and vulnerable than do pessimists (Tedeschi et al., 1993). These "neurotic" characteristics may interfere with abilities to produce growth or perceive benefits when confronting traumatic events.

So far, there is initial evidence that growth is more likely to be perceived among people who are more optimistic (Tedeschi & Calhoun, in press), and that perceiving growth increases optimism (Park, Cohen, & Murch, in press). However, the relationship between optimism and perceptions of growth are relatively low (correlations approximately .1 to .3), indicating that the tendency to experience growth is not "simply" optimism (Park et al., in press; Tedeschi & Calhoun, in press).

Hardiness

The hardiness personality style described by Kobasa (Kobasa, 1979; Kobasa, Maddi, Puccetti, & Zola, 1985) consists of tendencies toward *commitment, control,* and *challenge.* Committed people are curious and actively involved in what is to be done; those high in control believe that they can influence events; and those with a tendency toward challenge expect that life will confront them with changes that will stimulate personal development.

Lazarus and Folkman (1984) point out that strong commitments in particular areas of life create vulnerabilities in those areas. However, strong commitments may also yield attempts to reduce threat and sustain pursuit of goals in the face of obstacles that are commonplace in traumatic life events. Commitments to values and ideals tend to be emotionally laden, making it personally important to perceive meaning and benefit and find hope in situations that would otherwise be overwhelming. According to Kobasa, hardy people produce optimistic cognitive appraisals, perception of meaning in stressful events, and a willingness to learn something of value from these events and incorporate this into a life plan.

The hardiness construct has been studied most often in relation to ability to resist stressful events, and particularly physical illnesses (Hannah, 1988; Kobasa et al., 1985) that appear to be associated with these events (Maddi, Bartone, & Puccetti, 1987). This relationship may be the result of certain appraisal processes. In a stressful laboratory task, Wiebe (1991) found that hardy men appraised the task as less threatening and responded to it with less negative affect and physiological arousal and more positive affect, than those low in hardiness. Weaker effects of hardiness were found for women. Wiebe suggested that hardiness is related to both active coping responses and minimization of emotional distress. Manning, Williams, and Wolfe (1988) found that hardiness did not moderate the relationship between stressors and health, but discovered that hardy people reported more positive affect, energy, and a higher quality of life, along with fewer somatic complaints, less depression, and less anxiety, than did people low in hardiness.

It remains unclear whether commitment, control, or challenge is most responsible for the observed effects of hardiness. A univariate conceptualization of hardiness has been offered by Younkin (1992), who reported that hardiness is related to less psychiatric symptomatology and greater self-esteem. Among women, there was also a relationship between hardiness and lower levels of depression and higher self-reported autonomy. For the purposes of our understanding of the relationship between personality and perception of benefits from trauma, such findings suggest that hardiness is a buffer against stress and is associated with appraisals of threat that minimize emotional distress and promote active attempts at coping. Of course, hardiness, like locus of control and self-efficacy, may not be the best personality disposition under all traumatic circumstances (Swindle et al., 1988). Although these propensities may be associated with good outcomes in coping and perception of benefits, there is no research to date that draws a direct link from hardiness to personal growth or perception of benefits from trauma.

Resilience

Resilience is a concept that has been described by several authors who applied it to children who have endured a start to their lives that has put them at risk for life failures, but who have managed to succeed nonetheless (Baruch & Stutman, 1992; Beardslee & Podorefsky, 1988; Garmezy, 1985; Green, 1986; Rutter, 1987; Stutman & Baruch, 1992; Werner, 1984). Green (1986) describes resilience as an ability to accept one's own weakness while embarking on "achievable ventures" (p. 278). Beardslee and Podorefsky (1988), in a study of adolescents coping with parents suffering from serious psychiatric disorders, found that resilient adolescents were able to make accurate appraisals of the stress to be dealt with, of their own capacity to act and the consequences of those actions, and of their ability to function independently. Especially important was the ability to give up responsibility for parental illness and the hope that they could change it. This process of focusing on what aspects of problems can be fruitfully addressed may be important in generating perceptions of benefits.

Werner has been pursuing research with a sample of Hawaiian children at risk because of poor family circumstances (Werner, 1984, 1989; Werner & Smith, 1982). She reported four characteristics that these resilient children have in common: (a) an active problem-solving approach, (b) a tendency to perceive even painful experiences constructively, (c) an ability to gain other people's positive attention, and (d) an ability to maintain a sense of meaning in life through faith. They seemed to be able to find the strength to care for other people in need while also separating themselves from their troubles by engaging in pastimes they found enjoyable. From Werner's descriptions, one perceives these children as balanced in their abilities to be self-reliant and to pursue and find help and comfort when necessary. Resilient children have temperaments, personalities, or abilities to attract helpful, caring people to them.

Werner (1984) states that "for some children some stress appears to have a steeling rather than a scarring effect" (p. 71), but that the likelihood of the steeling may also have to do with the shifting balance between vulnerability and protective factors during the life cycle. Boys appear to be more vulnerable than girls when exposed to chronic and intense family discord during childhood, and girls are more vulnerable during adolescence. Furthermore, this resiliency is nurtured by others who model helping others and turning to others for help, and a conviction that life makes sense and that things work out, despite adversity. Resilience is not the result of temperament only; environmental influences are also crucial.

Rutter (1987) and Garmezy (1985) described both personality and environmental factors associated with resilience in children. The personality factors included self-esteem and self-efficacy. The environmental events leading to resilience may not be pleasant happenings, but rather stressors that are successfully engaged, resulting in additional strength (Holahan & Moos, 1990). Rutter (1987) describes such events as inoculations against future difficulty. He also notes that protective processes that lead to strengthening are crucial at key turning points rather than being long-standing attributes or experiences. This notion is similar to Bandura's (1982b) that both personal proclivities and environmental events, especially encounters with certain people, have a crucial effect at particular points in life. Perhaps resilient children not only are particularly capable of withstanding traumatic events but also have been created from some of the same forces in childhood that may produce positive changes in adults who face trauma as well. At turning points in life when trauma occurs, certain personal qualities may also be involved in reducing the possibility of negative chain reactions (Rutter, 1987), so that more adaptive, rather than maladaptive, patterns of response will occur. Rutter suggests that for children, qualities of "equable mood, malleability, predictability of behavior, mild to moderate intensity of emotional reactions . . . an approaching style to new situations . . . [and] a sense of humor" (p. 326) are all important in producing responses to difficulties that engage others rather than create further interpersonal difficulties. There is an interactive, cyclical nature of environmental events and personality that produces strengthening of children and movement onto beneficial life paths.

In their discussion of resilient children, Stutman and Baruch (1992) draw on Eriksonian developmental theory to highlight personality variables that they term "intrapsychic strengths," as well as environmental variables. The intrapsychic strengths include trust, self-regulation, autonomy, self-esteem, empathy, altruism, internal locus of control, flexibility, and optimism. Many of these characteristics, together with a facilitative environment and a "good fit" with a child's temperament, are seen to produce certain action-oriented coping skills. Such an action-oriented approach to coping is an important element that tends to produce perceptions of benefits such as the strength and perceived self-reliance discussed in Chapter 3. The interactive nature of environment, personality, and coping skills fits with the approaches of Bandura (1978) and Rutter (1987), as well as our understanding of the

complex interactions responsible for producing growth and perceptions of benefits in crises.

Green (1986) suggests that a central element in resilient children's
ability to manage their life difficulties is that they have a flexible
attributional style. Such a style allows for holding apparently contradictory notions about their power simultaneously: "I am powerless
over influencing these events, but I can still look after myself successfully during this confusion and crisis." Hurley (1987) has reported on
cognitive-behavioral programs used with children being treated for
cancer that encourage just this kind of attributional style. Children
learn to minimize the discomfort of treatment through some self-
control strategies and are then able to submit to it with much less
aggression and fear.

Sense of Coherence

In attempting to account for people who manage to stay well while
under conditions of stress, Antonovsky (1987) describes personal characteristics that, together with certain stressors, promote salutary outcomes. This "salutogenic," as opposed to pathogenic, orientation recog-
nizes that stress is omnipresent and can have benefits if responded to
appropriately. People who are in the best position to respond well to
stress have a "sense of coherence," which includes three components:
comprehensibility, manageability, and meaningfulness.

Comprehensibility refers to the expectation a person has that events,
whether desirable or not, will make cognitive sense and be orderly
and explicable. The opposite pole is described as noise; that is, events
are perceived to be disordered, random, accidental, and inexplicable.
For example, bereaved parents made mention of this during a group
discussion when they referred to the deaths of their children as
violating the natural order that their children should survive them.
Furthermore, the way these deaths occurred were not understandable.
How could an airplane be fine on one flight and crash on the next?
How could a person in a car die during an accident while another
person sitting next to him or her be unscathed? The order, structure,
and consistency of events that they expected seemed to be violated by
these deaths.

A second component of a sense of coherence is *manageability*. Some people see experiences in life as challenges that can be coped with or, at worst, that are bearable. At the opposite pole, people tend to see negative things as seeking them out, with life continually victimizing them. Antonovsky (1987) mentions that a central element in manageability is a sense that resources are at one's disposal to cope with events. These resources may be "under one's own control or . . . controlled by legitimate others—one's spouse, friends, colleagues, God, history, the party leader, a physician—whom one feels one can count on, whom one trusts" (pp. 17-18). Therefore, this concept goes beyond confidence in one's own coping ability to a faith that one way or another, through one kind of force or another, events will be tolerable.

Meaningfulness refers to a view that demands and challenges are worthy of investment and engagement, that meaning can be found even in undesirable events, and that one will continue to feel motivated to proceed even when significant difficulties arise. We will see that the search for the meaning of events is an important part of the process of construing benefits, and Antonovsky (1987) points out that certain people tend to be more adept at approaching events in this way. He sees meaningfulness as the most important component because without it, comprehensibility is unstable and one loses the motivation to continue to manage events. On the other hand, high meaningfulness drives a person to engage in a search for comprehensibility and the resources to manage events.

Although all of life does not have to be comprehensible, manageable, and meaningful to achieve a sense of coherence, there are four crucial spheres that must be seen as meaningful: inner feelings; interpersonal relationships; one's major activity; and existential issues such as death, failure, conflict, and isolation. Crises may produce benefits by ultimately shedding light on the meaning that can be recognized in one or more of these areas, even if events initially challenge their meaningfulness, comprehensibility, or manageability.

The "Big Five" Personality Factors

Personality has been described as having five components at its most general level of analysis: neuroticism, extroversion, openness, agreeableness, and conscientiousness (Costa & McCrae, 1985). Perceiving benefits appears to be associated with at least two of the five major factors of personality. Growth appears to be related to the personality trait of extroversion, particularly a tendency to be active and experience positive emotion, and to the tendency to be open to internal experience (Tedeschi & Calhoun, in press). Extroverted people are active, prefer to be involved with others, and feel positive emotions. Those people who are open to experience have been described as being able to appreciate and seek experiences, and being "curious, imaginative, and willing to entertain novel ideas" (Costa & Widiger, 1994, p. 3). The factors of agreeableness and conscientiousness have a weaker relationship with perceptions of benefit, and neuroticism appears to be unrelated (Tedeschi & Calhoun, in press).

A longitudinal study of personality (McCrae & Costa, 1993) suggests that these general personality traits exist before the traumatic events and endure relatively unchanged afterward. Personality characteristics might set the stage for perception of particular benefits. For example, in our study of personality characteristics and different kinds of perceptions of growth (Tedeschi & Calhoun, in press), people who reported perceiving new possibilities for their lives appeared to be open to their internal world and to the external world, invited experiences and insights, had positive affect, and were active. People who perceived others in a more positive light believed they had developed more understanding of others, responded more intimately in their relationships, had general characteristics of warmth and gregariousness, and, in addition, were open to their feelings, were active, and experienced positive affect.

Similar personality characteristics were found for those reporting gains in a perception of personal strength, and these people also reported feeling capable rather than panicked and hopeless in the face of difficulties. The tendency to report an enhanced appreciation of life was related to similar personality characteristics as seen with the other reported benefits: warmth, activity, positive emotions, and openness to feelings. The tendency to perceive spiritual change was also related to these personality characteristics, as well as gregariousness and a tendency to be conservative and not open to reexamining religious values. These people may have assimilated their negative experiences into their framework of religious beliefs, and in the process strengthened them.

Creative Copers: Common Themes

The common themes that run through the literature on personality and successful adaptation to life crises appear to be the willingness to take up challenge and a persistently active approach to experiences and problem solving. However, the general expectation of success may work best, at least in situations where there are realistic limits to achievement, when balanced by an ability to judge when effort is being wasted on unachievable goals and a willingness to accept certain aspects of a changed situation. Therefore, traumas in which there are limitations on one's ability to exert control in the situation, and restrictions on the reestablishment of the status quo ante, will favor those who have established such a balance and flexibility and who are able to generate creative solutions.

Strickland (1989) has discussed creativity in relation to self-efficacy, locus of control, hardiness, optimism, and related constructs. She describes creative people as having these characteristics and others that allow a letting go of conventional approaches to problems; a tendency to act on, rather than merely react to, the environment; and an ability to bring order out of chaos. Averill and Nunley (1992) similarly emphasize authenticity, novelty, and effectiveness as components of "emotional creativity." These characteristics also appear to be related to extroversion and openness to experience. An alertness to the environment and flexibility in dealing with it are hallmarks of these people as they creatively construe their world, make plans, and regulate their behavior within limits that they recognize. These people may also construe themselves in diverse, complex ways, so that when a role is lost or they fail, they experience only minor damage to their self-esteem (Hamilton, Greenberg, Pyszczynski, & Cather, 1993). This approach to life appears to be necessary in allowing people to derive beneficial perspectives and associated behaviors in response to negative events.

The relationship between the crisis events, personality characteristics, and successful coping with personal growth is complex. But growth seems more likely for people who are resilient, optimistic, and hardy, and who face life crises that represent irreversible changes, because a new level of adaptation must be achieved. The degree of negativity that a crisis holds for a person is not completely inherent in the crisis but is related to the characteristics of the person. Virtually identical situations overwhelm some people, whereas others are able to progress through them.

From our review of the descriptions of people who cope well with crises, it appears that certain personal characteristics interact with the negativity of the situation to determine the likelihood of successful coping. People who score in the "healthy" ranges on these personality dimensions are able to cope with greater adversity. But although these may be the people who are best able to overcome crises, they may have much less to gain from confronting crises, compared to people who perceive themselves to be somewhat less capable. People who are moderately capable on these dimensions, neither extremely poor at living skills and pessimistic about events and their ability to affect them, nor extremely competent and confident, may find the most benefit in successful coping with trauma. Although their coping may not measure up to that of the most hardy, resilient, and creative people, they have potential for significant growth.

We may expect a curvilinear relationship between these personal characteristics that we summarize as competence and confidence, and personal growth from coping with trauma. People who have poor coping skills and perceive themselves as less capable are likely to be overwhelmed by crises and unable to marshal any very effective response. Outcomes are therefore likely to be grim, and under such conditions, recognizable benefits are unlikely. However, people who are extremely capable are less likely to be challenged by most events, and therefore may perceive little or no change in their coping responses or understanding about how best to react. Perhaps only in the most extreme circumstances are these remarkably adaptive people likely to be stretched to their limits of coping, having to create new understandings and responses in order to manage. There may also be a ceiling effect, where little else can be gained in the realm of mental health and coping skills beyond a certain point. On the other hand, people with moderate levels of coping skill have much to gain and still have some ability to gain it. People who are healthy but have some room to grow into being more creative responders to significant traumas may benefit most from these events, although they may be at some risk for the negative outcomes described in Chapter 2.

This process of gaining from crisis among people with varying coping capabilities may be similar to the effects of physical challenges on people of varying degrees of physical fitness. At the peak of fitness, additional capabilities represent very small improvements gained under difficult training. Those who are very unfit can barely respond to the smallest demand and are discouraged by it immediately. Those people in the average range of fitness can rely on some capabilities to respond to physical exertion with some success and confidence, and therefore may continue to confront the physical challenges directly, promoting increases in fitness. There is evidence, in fact, that the creative approach to coping with trauma has positive effects on physical as well as emotional functioning, including immune system response (Bandura, Cioffi, Taylor, & Brouillard, 1988; Bandura, O'Leary, Taylor, Gauthier, & Gossard, 1987), resistance to cancer relapse (Levy, 1985), and increased catecholamine capacity (Dienstbier, 1992).

In the next chapter, we will focus on the thought processes that people use to deal with trauma and that tend to promote personal growth and the perception of benefit. We will then tie together our discussion of personality characteristics with events and processes that promote benefit in a general model presented in Chapter 6.

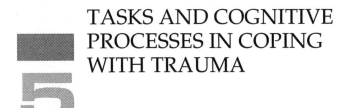

TASKS AND COGNITIVE PROCESSES IN COPING WITH TRAUMA

Cancer is a cosmic slap in the face. You either get discouraged or ennobled by it.

—Richard Belzer

In this chapter, we consider the main tasks that confront those people who are facing traumatic events. We will examine the cognitive strategies that enable people confronting trauma to complete these tasks and to formulate adaptive behavior that will address other tasks that require specific action. In the process of working on these tasks, people find the benefits to which we have referred in Chapter 3. The event itself is less important than the factors that influence how it is experienced in determining its psychological impact.

The variety of tasks that lay the foundation for positive changes and that are made necessary by traumatic events fall into three categories: manageability, comprehensibility, and meaningfulness. This terminology is derived from Antonovsky's (1987) discussion of "sense of coherence" (see Chapter 4) and maintenance of physical health and is related to themes of meaning, mastery, and self-esteem enhancement discussed by Taylor (1983). Tasks that are used to cope with trauma are interrelated, and movement through each category affects success in the others. We will describe each set of tasks and the cognitive mechanisms that allow successful processing of these tasks. Successful processing is often accompanied by the experience that something has been gained in the struggle to cope.

Rumination

As an ongoing feature of making the crisis manageable and comprehensible, as well as giving it meaning, individuals engage in the process of rumination. People who react to trauma ruminate on, or attempt to work through, the traumatic events. This is especially true of their early responses to trauma. Rumination has been described as a general response tendency that increases with the degree of stress and negative emotion (Horowitz, 1975, 1976). The process of *denial* alternates with the intrusive thoughts so that people give themselves doses of information as they are able to assimilate them (Janoff-Bulman, 1989a; Krystal, 1988). For some people, a "healthy denial" may allow adaptive coping over a long period of time (Druss & Douglas, 1988). Rumination is believed to subside as the person comes to terms with the trauma, that is, as the person is able to manage it, understand it, and find it meaningful, although the time it takes for this to occur is often much longer than has been assumed (Wortman & Silver, 1989). In a study of people who had endured a traumatic event between 2 and 50 years previously (Tait & Silver, 1989), frequent unintended, intrusive, and vivid ruminations still occurred. Except for positive emotions, which occurred more often in association with these ruminations over time, there was no clear change in other characteristics of ruminations over time. A form of this may even endure over a lifetime in successful copers. Whiteman (1993) describes the "two-track" thinking of Holocaust survivors who have been living successful and contented lives. They are usually able to compartmentalize memories of horror and the associated affect, enabling them to get on with their lives. However, certain situations can act as triggers, and images and feelings associated with the war temporarily flood them.

The contents of rumination include a review of the negative implications of events, a search for meaning, a feeling that one must discuss this event with others (Tait & Silver, 1989), and troubleshooting the frustration of attempts to achieve important goals (Martin & Tesser, 1989). Goals can be thought of as the achievement of a particular desired state, such as rebuilding one's home after it has burned or restoring one's self-esteem after a rape. Rumination increases when initial strategies of problem solving fail, producing a search for alternative means to achieve goals (Martin, Tesser, & McIntosh, 1993). Rumination also arises from an inability to decide on a course of action (Lazarus & Folkman, 1984).

Martin and Tesser (1989) describe goals as existing in a hierarchy of importance and abstraction. Under circumstances that do not allow achievement of goals, examination of these goals may ensue. Such rumination allows the person to disengage from unattainable goals. Substitution of the unattainable goal with another may be important to avoid disruption of the goal hierarchy and frustration of very important higher-order goals. This process involves *suppressing competing activities* in order to focus on, rather than be distracted by, other concerns (Carver, Scheier, & Weintraub, 1989). A musician suffering a stroke may choose to give up playing for a while to concentrate on physical rehabilitation. Restraint may be necessary to time actions to produce the best effect. The musician has to wait until enough progress has been made in rehabilitation before playing his or her instrument again. It may be that some goals are unattainable at present, or less important given the circumstances. They may be taken up again later after certain aspects of current circumstances have been successfully addressed.

If rumination has continued for a long period of time, there will be an extensive pattern of associations connected with the unattained goal. Thoughts about the goal and its frustration are then frequently cued from the environment as a result of the network of associations. Rumination can be ended by the clear identification of the goal and its abandonment or substitution.

Making the Crisis Manageable

All individuals confronting life crises need to appraise the degree to which events are threatening (Lazarus & Folkman, 1984) and find some way to reverse the negative changes that have occurred. But most crises are not reversible, or reversible only to some degree. This is one of the reasons that events are appraised as traumatic in the first place. When confronted with trauma, a person initially may believe that a return to the status quo is possible. However, that person may come to recognize that this is not possible. As a result of a process of overcoming initial denial that something has been lost, people begin to define the tasks before them, deciding on what is possible and what is manageable. People who suffer injuries attempt to heal and regain physical and mental functions; those who lose their belongings in natural disasters or through crime attempt to replace them; those who lose their jobs try to find new ones; the bereaved attempt to replace the lost loved one with other people who can assume similar roles in their lives. Definition of appropriate tasks is not usually a smooth or rapid process. It involves a series of steps in overcoming denial, and allowing certain information to be considered and other tasks and goals to be put aside.

PRIMARY AND SECONDARY CONTROL

If instrumental activity is seen as possible and justified by suffi-ciently important potential benefits, then a great deal of effort at reversing or improving the situation can be expected (Rotter, 1954; Stotland, 1969). Jerry, the paralyzed man quoted in Chapter 1, initially expended a great deal of energy trying to walk again, practicing with leg braces, walkers, and other devices. If these attempts at "primary control" (Rothbaum, Weisz, & Snyder, 1982) fail to reverse the crisis situation or its aftermath, there is likely to be a decreased sense of self-efficacy on the part of the person. People who have demonstrated self-efficacy in the past—those with resilient, hardy, or optimistic personalities—are likely to find this intolerable.

The process through which people experiencing trauma go in de-termining for themselves the degree to which they have control over their lives often leads to what appears to be self-blame (Brickman et al., 1982). People often blame themselves for their predicament, but this may be seen as an attempt to maintain the notion that they are responsible for outcomes and may be able to continue to produce changes in their new life situation. Self-blame, or internal attributions of blame, are most likely to lead to positive outcomes when the trauma was avoidable (Brewin, 1984) and the blame is placed on one's specific behavior rather than on one's character (Janoff-Bulman, 1979). This is probably because the person can then perceive different choices under his or her control and can produce better outcomes in the future.

People give up beliefs in primary control when these beliefs produce too much disappointment (Rothbaum et al., 1982). This will lead to such behaviors as passivity, withdrawal, and submissiveness. The aversiveness of disappointment will be overcome by developing a more accurate prediction of the outcome of events so that one will not be caught off guard. For example, an adolescent girl who contracted polio went through a number of steps in overcoming denial and giving up primary control over a period of 2 years after her paralysis. These steps involved adjusting the time needed for full recovery further and further into the future, until a doctor told her to adjust to a sedentary life. The reality of her situation became clear:

> I wasn't ignoring it. I was relieved. It took much less energy than that damned two-year plan. And I was depressed. . . . I had moved through one level of acknowledgement—facing the facts—only to find myself immediately embroiled in a struggle with a second level—acceptance of the implications. (Vash, 1981, p. 126)

Such an adjustment to uncontrollable events involves the development of "secondary control," an adjustment of expectations to a difficult environment to reduce unpredictability, disappointment, and stress. This secondary control may appear as an *acceptance*, as opposed to a denial (Carver, Scheier, & Weintraub, 1989), of unchangeable aspects of a situation, or acceptance of one's limited capacity to produce certain changes. *Behavioral disengagement* and *mental disengagement* are processes that involve, respectively, giving up attempts to attain certain goals and distracting oneself from goals that are difficult to give up. However, these may be dysfunctional coping strategies (Carver, Scheier, & Weintraub, 1989). Setting aside too many goals can lead to apathy and depression.

Among those people who perceive self-efficacy and are seeking primary control, only long and chronic conditions of uncontrollability are likely to produce giving up. At this juncture, a proper balance of primary and secondary control must be attained. The best adjustment may be achieved when people learn how and when to use the processes of primary and secondary control and integrate them (Rothbaum et al., 1982). The achievement of secondary control often involves searching for meaning and understanding.

USE OF RELIGIOUS BELIEFS

For many people, crises can be made more manageable by reliance on religious beliefs, in which God or related concepts play a central role. There are varying approaches to the "use" of religion in coping with negative life events. For people with worldviews that include religious metaphysical assumptions, a "deferring" style tends to stress external support from God. People who feel confident in confronting personal problems may be more likely to develop a "self-directing" style, in which God plays a relatively minor role, or a "collaborative" style, involving an active, personal exchange with God (Pargament et al., 1988).

The deferring style can be an obstacle to opportunities for learning, whereas the collaborative style helps people manage anxiety and other emotions while encouraging active explorations of the world and the development of more effective living skills. However, there are certain traumatic events that are better approached with one style or another, and these styles may not be mutually exclusive. The collaborative style may provide the most opportunities for individuals to feel supported while engaging in problem solving (Spilka, 1989). God is at their side while they help themselves, and this may be how spiritual support helps to maintain self-esteem (Maton, 1989). The collaborative style also allows for a more comfortable acceptance of secondary control when necessary, as certain aspects of problems may be left in God's hands.

VICARIOUS LEARNING

The initial attempts at primary control can be encouraged by the observation of the success of others and the accompanying vicarious reinforcement (Bandura, 1978) or avoidance of negative outcomes observed in others suffering similar crises (Veronen & Kilpatrick, 1983). One of the reasons people seek social support is to learn how to cope effectively and avoid pitfalls (Carver, Scheier, & Weintraub, 1989). New behaviors are more likely to be performed when the observer also witnesses reinforcements being obtained by the model as a result of performing these behaviors (Bandura, 1978). This process may be important in crises and their aftermath when behaviors not in a victim's repertoire may enable successful adjustment. For example, disabled people may have to learn many new techniques for negotiating the physical environment that were irrelevant to them when they were able-bodied.

One difficulty with the necessity of observing others to achieve a more positive adjustment is that the circumstances of the victim may be different enough from the model's that the model's behaviors are not appropriate for the situation of the person in crisis, and may therefore lead to failure to adjust. Also, these observations may not only provide information about the possibilities for successful coping, but at the same time lead to the conclusion that one is worse off than others (i.e., the "upward comparison"), which may then lead to negative consequences for adjustment.

DOWNWARD SOCIAL COMPARISONS

The aftermath of trauma can be cognitively managed by the process of "selective evaluation," by which people cognitively manage their victimization (Taylor, Wood, & Lichtman, 1983). The status of "victim" is so aversive that after crises, steps are taken to minimize "victimization." One step is the downward social comparison. Others are perceived as worse off than oneself, enhancing self-esteem and increasing distance between the self and other victims (Perloff & Fetzer, 1986).

Wills (1987) describes a range of passive and active methods of downward comparison. Survivors of trauma may imagine worse possible outcomes and see themselves as fortunate: "It could have been a lot worse." They may notice less fortunate others (e.g., "there but for the grace of God") in presentations by the media, allowing downward comparisons, and may assume that their positive attributes are relatively rare and their negative ones commonplace. They may focus on particular others who are coping less well or who are worse off in a particular way, or attribute negative traits to others, actively derogating them. Downward comparisons are more likely to be effective in enhancing life satisfaction and decreasing anxiety and depression than are upward comparisons (Gibbons, 1986; Wills, 1987), and, perhaps for this reason, they are favored by people experiencing trauma (Wood, Taylor, & Lichtman, 1985). Downward comparisons may also reduce the belief that one's experience in crisis is rare or exclusive, providing some relief from rumination about why one was singled out for catastrophe (Taylor, Wayment, & Collins, 1993).

REDUCING EMOTIONAL DISTRESS

In the above discussion, we have been attending to coping processes that allow someone facing a crisis or its aftermath to solve problems associated with loss. But there are also important tasks that involve reducing emotional distress. A person who is raped may struggle to overcome fear of vulnerability; bereaved people may attempt to escape the pain of grief; those who become physically disabled must leave behind much of the anger and resentment of being unable to easily perform many activities. At the time when crises are initially experienced, people do not conceive of positive outcomes or psychological growth, but are preoccupied by attempting to replace or recover what has been lost, if possible, and to reduce the distressing emotions brought on by these events. Only through the relief of some of this distress does growth become possible (Kast, 1990).

As described in Chapter 2, emotional distress, including anxiety, depression, and physical changes, is so extreme in most people experiencing major crises that it may first produce psychic numbing, and later almost unbearable emotional pain. Therefore, relief of emotional distress becomes a crucial task. This emotion-focused coping (Lazarus & Folkman, 1984) can interact with attempts to reverse the calamity, in that relief of emotional distress allows for more productive problem solving and vice versa.

A fairly straightforward coping mechanism is *venting of emotions*, which may be connected with *seeking support for emotional reasons* (Carver, Scheier, & Weintraub, 1989). Whether these strategies are useful depends on when they are employed after the traumatic event. Expression of emotion can be beneficial early on, but continued focus on emotion is counterproductive later if it is experienced as beyond one's control (Tait & Silver, 1989). There are individual differences in the degree to which people believe they can control emotional responses (Wasch & Kirsch, 1992). Decisions about when to be emotional or allow oneself to consider threatening aspects of a situation may reflect shifts in appraisals of personal control as certain aspects of the situation vary over time (Folkman, 1984). This active, thoughtful approach to dealing with threats is a tool that people can use to cope effectively with a variety of future situations.

The simple initial goals of getting back to something approaching normalcy in what life provides and how one feels can ultimately produce changes that go far beyond this. The struggle involved in reaching some initial goals and giving up others appears to be at least partially responsible for the positive changes that occur following trauma. In trying to overcome their "victim" status, people are stretched to the limits of their ability to endure physical and psychological pain, anxiety, patience, anger, and sadness. It has been said that anything that does not kill you will make you stronger, and somehow there may be a match between the fortitude and skills of the person and the degree of negativity in the event, which combine to produce benefits. However, people in the midst of crises are almost never interested in such things because of their emotional distress and the apparently overwhelming nature of their problems. The benefits may be seen only in retrospect.

Making the Crisis Comprehensible

SCHEMAS: BASIC ASSUMPTIONS ABOUT LIFE

Life is comprehensible because as individuals, we bring order to the chaos through a conceptual system that provides expectations about ourselves and the world that allow us to act and respond with some confidence. The idea that people construct templates for reality or make implicit probability statements about events, and act accordingly, has been found in many psychological theories (e.g., Epstein, 1973; Kelly, 1955; Parkes, 1971; Rotter, 1954; Stotland, 1969). The organized cognitive structures that serve as theories on which to base our processing of information—including attention, memory, meaning, planning, and, ultimately, action—have been referred to as *schemas* (Anderson, 1985; Fiske & Taylor, 1984; Hastie, 1981). Schemas are related to each other hierarchically.

Perhaps the most supraordinate schema is described by McCann and Pearlman (1990) as the *frame of reference*. This is comprised of attributions of causality, locus of control, and hopefulness. Higher-order schemas have also been described as relating to fundamental issues about our self-worth and power; the benevolence of others, including issues of trust, safety, and intimacy; and meaning (Epstein, 1980; McCann & Pearlman, 1990). Lower-order schemas have to do with more specific issues, such as our competence in mathematics. To modify or replace higher-order, fundamental schemas is a difficult task because lower-order, specific assumptions are dependent on them.

Our particular ways of making the world comprehensible to ourselves—the schemas or assumptions we hold—are resistant to change. This is understandable if we recognize that our world depends quite literally on these schemas. Without them, we cannot think clearly or comprehend and react to events around us. Wuthnow (1992) describes our everyday reality—based on attending to only a sliver of all the possible stimulation and facts, and built on illusions that allow "haunting suspicions" to be pushed aside as we deal with the tasks of the moment.

> It is a routine world, an orderly world in which things have their place. Deeper questions . . . are minimized. Everyday reality is also a safe, secure world in which we know our place and can largely take for granted the objects and persons in our immediate environment. (Wuthnow, 1992, p. 15)

Implied are the basic needs and corresponding basic belief dimensions, such as beliefs in a benevolent world populated by people we can count on; a comprehensible, predictable, and meaningful world; and a worthy self. The maintenance of these beliefs or positive illusions (Taylor & Brown, 1988) allows the world to remain comprehensible and stable in our eyes. This allows for the possibility that we can control or manage it in much of our daily living, and opens the possibility that living may be meaningful or that we can make it so.

According to terror management theory, higher-order schemas, such as the belief that good members of the society will have good fortune, tend to be cultural beliefs that allow us to manage the otherwise paralyzing fears of death. Therefore, we cultivate self-esteem to buffer ourselves against vulnerability (Hamilton et al., 1993). It is no wonder that we cling to our schemas. We are willing to give up marriages before giving up self-concept, a higher-order schema (Parkes, 1971).

TRAUMAS AS CHALLENGES TO SCHEMAS

But higher-order schemas can be challenged by traumatic events, calling into question our basic assumptions about ourselves and the world (Epstein, 1990), therefore making life difficult to comprehend. Victimizing events may dramatically challenge an individual's fundamental assumptions about the degree to which people are benevolent, one's self-worth, and the comprehensibility of events (Janoff-Bulman, 1989a, 1992). One suggestion has been to consider comprehensibility as centered around the beliefs that good and bad things happen on the basis of certain distributional principles: (a) Some people are deserving, and get what they deserve; (b) people's behavior determines what happens to them; or (c) chance or randomness prevails, and there is nothing one can do to affect what will happen (Janoff-Bulman, 1989a). Comparing people who had experienced one or more of a variety of traumatic events with people who had not had such experiences, Janoff-Bulman (1989a) reported that those who had experienced trauma saw the world as less benevolent, and themselves less positively. Effects of this kind may persist for many years (Silver & Wortman, 1980).

During the primary appraisal process, when people are first determining how threatening an event may be, many people find that the event they are confronting is incomprehensible. This initial reaction is well-known as *denial* (Carver, Scheier, & Weintraub, 1989). When people admit to the reality of the event, *acceptance* takes its place. We are referring to denial and acceptance here in relation to the reality of the entire circumstance rather than in relation to the possibility of certain coping responses, as mentioned above. The movement from denial to acceptance is not necessarily a smooth or rapid one. Much of the process of rumination discussed above appears to be in the service of attempting to assimilate the new information about the world and the self into existing schemas. People who clearly recognize the reality of their circumstances will still sometimes get the feeling that they cannot believe this happened to them.

When initially confronted with major life trauma, people tend to feel overwhelmed by the environment, as well as helpless. They are particularly aware and reactive to environmental events, and a great deal of information may be taken in, although only later can it be understood and used. The comprehensibility of the world suffers because people have difficulty taking a detached, nonsubjective perspective. The complexity of the concepts that they use to understand people is reduced, and they have difficulty with constructing ways to understand causal relationships (Healy, 1989; Stewart, 1982).

As we attempt to make crises comprehensible, there can be substantial variability in how we see ourselves, who we might become, and how we view the likelihood of our success in pursuing life plans and goals. But after the initial breakdown of existing schemas, which produces difficulty in the processing of information, later, perhaps over a period of years, the new experiences are integrated into revised schemas, "promoting long-term beneficial changes in cognitive processing" (Healy, 1989, p. 125). For Holocaust survivors, a crucial factor in how well they adjusted after the war was their ability to assimilate the knowledge that they survived the horror, whereas millions of others did not (Helmreich, 1992). Both positive and negative changes in views of self, world, and the future have been reported in cancer patients, who also felt much more positive about their relationships and life priorities (Collins et al., 1990). This suggests that a substantial reorganization of schemas may occur as a result of significant trauma. Chronic trauma may tend to produce more generalized, higher-order schemas rather than specific changes in assumptions. In one study, chronic family conflict was associated with negative assumptions about the benevolence of others and the world, whereas parental divorce without chronic conflict was associated with more pessimism specific to marriage (Franklin, Janoff-Bulman, & Roberts, 1990). Certain higher-order, basic assumptions were maintained, whereas the schema for marriage was altered.

Finding That Life
Continues to Be Meaningful

Different authors use the term "meaningfulness" to encompass a varying range of issues that are fundamental to making sense out of life and guiding our behavior (Antonovsky, 1987; Frankl, 1963; Janoff-Bulman, 1989a). Meaning has been said to allow us to perceive patterns (Baumeister, 1991), guide our actions, and regulate our behavior and emotions (Baumeister, 1991; Janoff-Bulman, 1989a). These functions more appropriately fall within the task of manageability discussed earlier in this chapter.

We see finding meaning in life as something beyond finding life manageable or comprehensible. Meaning imbues life with value and purpose, making it worth an emotional commitment. Meaningfulness

> refers to the extent to which one feels that life makes sense emotionally, that at least some of the problems and demands posed by living are worth investing energy in, are worthy of commitment and engagement, and are challenges that are "welcome" rather than burdens that one would much rather do without. (Antonovsky, 1987, p. 19)

Finding meaning is not, of course, a task confronted only by people who are suffering. This is an existential issue faced by us all. Existentialists assume that there is no inherent meaning in events or life; rather, life is imbued with meaning by each individual. Many of us have not worked out an elaborate metaphysical system. Baumeister (1991) suggests that, instead, meaning is imposed by individuals gradually, in small bits, using broad frameworks offered by their culture as contexts for their attempts to make sense of things. What people have as a system of meaning is a work in progress.

Cognitive theorists suggest that schemas are the constructions that provide the meaning to events. In particular, it is the higher-order schemas that are involved in construing meaning. As we have discussed in relation to comprehensibility, these same schemas can be challenged by trauma, may fail to provide meaning to traumatic events, or may need to be modified to give new meaning to events and to life. Finding meaning in life despite the impact of trauma actually involves two somewhat different tasks. One task involves finding meaning in the occurrence of the traumatic event itself, whereas the other task involves the maintenance of a view that life is meaningful despite the occurrence of the event. Some people may continue to find life as a whole meaningful even though the traumatic event they have suffered seems meaningless. Others may find meaning in both the traumatic event, or its aftermath, and life as a whole. Still others may not find meaning anywhere.

The importance of maintaining or finding meaning in traumatic events has been demonstrated in a number of studies. In one study, bereaved people were less likely to believe in a meaningful world than were the nonbereaved, and grief was less intense among bereaved people who did find meaning in the event. Specifically, the meaning found was an answer to the question about why the event occurred. Explanations included references to the health habits of the deceased, God's will, and the potential beneficial effects the death could have (Schwartzberg & Janoff-Bulman, 1991).

When meaning is found, it appears that the meaning is positive in some sense. In a study of people whose homes were destroyed by fire (Thompson, 1985), this was also found to be the case. Better outcomes in terms of less emotional distress and more active problem solving were associated with the ability to find meaning. It may be that finding meaning is easier within existing higher-order schemas, especially if such fundamental assumptions are not empirically disconfirmable. If all events can be understood and life can retain its value, no matter how traumatic the event, because of the belief in a higher-order assumption, even the most traumatic circumstances may be tolerated (Hamilton et al., 1993). For people who do not have higher-order schemas that can assimilate the traumatic event, the attempts to find meaning in these events may promote the development of these schemas.

RELIGIOUS ROUTES TO MEANING

Religion can provide higher-order schemas that can serve to preserve meaning in life even when events themselves seem senseless and tragic. Varying responses to the challenge to these schemas were reported in a study of cancer patients and parents of children with cancer. About two thirds of the patients became more religious after the diagnosis of cancer, whereas one third became less religious, often as a result of feeling betrayed by God (Spilka, 1989).

To prevent traumatic events from shaking foundations of meaning, the individual's sense of purpose and value must be universal and enduring. Traumatic events are difficult to absorb because they can shatter an important illusion that we nurture—that certain things are permanent. When important beliefs or relationships are lost or threatened, a source of continuing permanence and stability is useful (Baumeister, 1991). Because religion deals in universal truth and enduring values, it can preserve meaning in the face of the violation of other illusions of permanence or invulnerability—that we can ward off disease; that our children will survive us; and that our homes, jobs, and fortunes are secure against crime or natural disaster (Calhoun et al., 1992). As one bereaved parent remarked, "If I didn't believe in the resurrection, nothing would any longer make sense." Religion has been described as an all-embracing order that maintains itself and shelters us from chaos: a "sacred canopy" (Berger, 1967). This higher-order schema is adaptive when it leads to positive affect and the confidence to "engage in new behaviors, to test one's limits, and to maximize the possibilities of one's success" (Janoff-Bulman, 1989b, p. 169). Certainly, this is a constructive way to address traumatic events.

The meaning that religion offers in the face of chaos also can be applied to the traumatic events themselves. These events can be interpreted as being part of a universal plan; a prophecy; a divine punishment, test, or message; or have some other connection with the motives of God, especially when God is viewed as benign (Pargament et al., 1991). It appears that people do not often use religion to account for everyday events but may rely on it when confronting important, emotionally intense experiences (Lupfer, Brock, & DePaola, 1992). In these situations, some people often cite God's will as an explanation (Pargament et al., 1990). In making such interpretations, people may be implicitly minimizing the dramatic and powerful effects of the events by incorporating them into something much larger. Through this incorporation into the divine, the events have meaning that is no longer personal and impermanent but universal and enduring. This can be accomplished in a passive way by assuming that there must be some part of God's will being acted out, or that the events can be given spiritual significance in a more active way by increasing one's devotion or religious activity.

Action can serve to make events seem more manageable, but activity may be easier to engage in when it is meaningful to the actor.

Religion offers particular activities that are prescribed on certain occasions. These rituals and the religious institutions that support them have a firm connection with what is enduring, and therefore can be powerful ways of providing meaning to what is disruptive and extraordinary (Wuthnow, 1992). They can provide an outlet for emotional expression, offer social support, and offer activity that can make a situation feel more controllable and predictable (Pargament et al., 1991), protecting people with religious beliefs against the most negative aspects of traumatic events (Hall, 1986; Wortman & Silver, 1990).

BENEFITS OF RELIGIOUS MEANINGS

Interpretive control (Rothbaum et al., 1982) is a form of secondary control that is exerted when a religious meaning is given to events. For example, when God is viewed as producing the events for some purpose in one's life, this interpretation may allow for the acceptance of the event. *Vicarious secondary control* also may be enhanced by religious belief and activity, especially prayer. Petitioning God for help occurs within a faith that meaning still exists, that God is a positive force, that one still means something to God, and that one can control events through petitions to God. Meaning can therefore allow other constructive coping processes and outcomes, and there is substantial evidence that religion provides not only meaning but a basis for coping with emotional distress (Koenig, George, & Siegler, 1988), problem solving (Newman & Pargament, 1990; Pargament et al., 1990), and warding off alienation through social support (Pargament et al., 1991).

Maintenance of meaning or finding new meaning tends to be associated with maintenance of self-esteem, control, and positive views of the world and others (Spilka, 1989). Among parents whose infants died, finding meaning was associated with better adjustment immediately and 18 months after the loss (McIntosh, 1991). Parents for whom religion was important engaged in more "cognitive processing" or rumination—facilitating thinking about the loss, and finding meaning—although the rumination may temporarily produce more event-related distress before finally yielding increases in personal growth (Park & Cohen, 1993). There is also evidence (McIntosh, 1991) that the centrality and flexibility of the religious schema positively affect coping and that a well-developed schema that accounts for or allows a person to understand a traumatic event will be changed less by the event than will a poorly developed schema because it can be assimilated by the existing framework (Calhoun et al., 1992). Thus, traumatic events may appear meaningful only when highest-order schemas are changed a little or not at all, rather than when events shatter the framework of assumptions and understandings that a person holds.

The evidence to date suggests that when trauma throws into question the explicit or implicit meaning of life that a person has developed, the event may be perceived as meaningful to the extent that it provokes the development of new meanings. These new meanings may be found when people have to reorder their schemas, their behavior, or both. On the other hand, people may be able to live with the meaninglessness of a traumatic event, if life as a whole continues to be meaningful. Events may be seen as being less meaningful, and less traumatic, when they do not call into question a framework for the meaning of life, although they may be "meaningful" events in the sense that they provoked emotional reactions.

A final step in the process of giving meaning to traumatic events may be the weaving of these events into the life story or narrative in a way that gives them a central role, a crossroads where the path was taken to new insights about living (Harvey, Weber, & Orbuch, 1990; Thompson & Janigian, 1988). Individuals who successfully accomplish this task tend to make better adjustments to their circumstances (Harvey, Orbuch, Chwalisz, & Garwood, 1991).

Conclusions

We have described the interrelated tasks of manageability, comprehensibility, and meaningfulness that confront people coping with traumatic life events. Coping strategies mentioned throughout the literature are related to these general tasks in complex ways. Events that make these tasks so difficult that they challenge basic schemas about self, other people, and the world set the stage for a process of rumination. This rumination, which is usually accompanied by significant levels of psychological distress, provides the foundation from which new "insights" about life can emerge. As a result of the struggle, survivors of trauma leap beyond what they would have been without the challenge of the event and its aftermath, and experience a profound deepening of or change in their beliefs. This deepening or change is experienced as wisdom, rather than negativity. In turn, this wisdom guides them to new ways of relating to others and making life choices.

HOW GROWTH HAPPENS

A Model for Coping With Trauma

Maybe there is a plan for me to do something important before I die. I think God was trying to get the message through that it's time to get started.

—Eric Larsen, survivor of shark attack

In this chapter, we will "put the pieces together." We will consider personality and the tasks and processes of coping, and how these relate to three broad categories of perceived benefits that many persons see as having arisen out of their struggle with trauma: self-confidence, enhanced personal relationships, and changed philosophy of life. The focus of this chapter moves beyond successful coping with negative events to an accounting for how people appear to become strengthened by their coping with these events. Many useful models have been proposed to describe the coping process in general (Lazarus & Folkman, 1984) and the search for meaning in particular (Baumeister, 1991), but there has been no specific attempt to describe the process of growth and the perception of positive change following trauma.

Other researchers in this area (e.g., Lazarus & Folkman, 1984; Scheier, Weintraub, & Carver, 1986) have considered the perception of growth to be a coping process of positive reinterpretation rather than an outcome of coping. However, the experience of persons who make these "positive reinterpretations," based on their explanations in their own words, is that certain benefits were an outcome of their attempts to cope with trauma. We will take this perspective and describe how these benefits arise. A model of this process has been described by Schaefer and Moos (1992) that includes the "environmental system" (essentially, supportive others), the "personal system" (i.e., demographic and personal characteristics), the event itself, and the appraisal and coping responses used. According to Schaefer and Moos, the positive outcomes are categorized as enhancements in social relationships; coping skills; and understanding of self, others, and principles of living. Our model includes these elements of the process and outcome along with other details. Before presenting our model, let us consider a number of principles that are involved in the process of personal growth in the aftermath of trauma.

Principle 1: Growth Occurs
When Schemas Are Changed by Traumatic Events

This principle is based on the assumption that people actively construct an understanding or model of reality (Kelly, 1955; Neimeyer, 1993). This model is a cognitive organization that must be preserved over time to allow a person access to the stored information (Greenwald, 1980). The schemas (i.e., assumptions of optimistic outcomes, the centrality of self, and the occurrence of only certain expected events) are preserved but are not static. The process of constructing the schemas used to explain and predict events is continuous. Trauma is a severe disruption in this ongoing process. The organized schemas may become disorganized by trauma, producing an attempt to re-create a useful system; at the least, negative events may produce additions to the schemas because such traumas were previously incomprehensible or unimaginable (Janoff-Bulman, 1992). Because the schemas used to construct a model of the self and world provide the individual with ways of making the world comprehensible, meaningful, and manageable, trauma exposes the individual to the distressing thought that things are no longer comprehensible, meaningful, or manageable.

Traumas do not simply expose our schemas to the harsh realities, but produce new schemas. New assumptions or beliefs are not exactly new, however. They may have already existed as part of a fragmented schematic system in which contradictory notions are simultaneously held or at least known about because of awareness of cultural myths and alternative beliefs held by others. For example, during the Midwest flooding of 1993, a group of incarcerated drug dealers applied superhuman efforts in an attempt to save a small Iowa town. Their efforts failed, but their superintendent asked them to remember this experience to bolster the notion that one persists even when the odds are poor. An existing fragment of a more socialized schema may have been activated to produce this persistent, selfless effort in these criminals. Traumatic events may activate some less clearly defined or frequently used fragment of the cognitive system (Kelly, 1955). The fragment may then become a dominant schema. Development or maturation may be a sequence of replacements of beliefs (e.g., the apparent invulnerability of youth replaced by the apparent acceptance of death by the elderly), or even the widening of the cognitive system to allow for more apparently contradictory elements to be held simultaneously. Traumas tend to force this development along a much more rapid time frame.

People are usually aware that traumatic things do happen, of course. Family and friends have been observed to have gone through difficulties, and strangers who are suffering are shown in the media. These vicarious experiences may provide some inoculation against trauma to the extent that they are seen as potentially relevant to one's own life. "Imbibing absurdity in small doses may hopefully build up a degree of immunity against it" (Fisher & Fisher, 1993, p. 193). Some events can present doses of challenge great enough to highlight the randomness, injustice, meaninglessness, and absurdity of things, but small enough for us to learn to tolerate it. Brief looks into existential absurdities may be helpful (Fisher & Fisher, 1993), and some individuals may be able to tolerate a moderate level of immersion in these absurdities, especially those persons with a certain degree of structure and support in their lives. But if a person is prone to practice the illusion of invulnerability, to assume "that can't happen here, or to me," these inoculations will not be powerful enough to serve as learning experiences for dealing with traumas when they do occur.

Furthermore, the personal experience of emotional distress that accompanies traumatic events makes them qualitatively different from the vicarious experiences. Although we are emphasizing cognitive changes in the model presented here, it should be understood that these changes occur as a result of tremendous emotional distress. The emotional element can set in motion the cognitive events that ultimately produce growth. Both affective and cognitive schemas are activated and integrated when successful coping occurs (Rybash, Hoyer, & Roodin, 1986).

A traumatic event often produces shock and denial as initial defenses against the emotional distress that is otherwise felt. This reaction is associated with the illusion of invulnerability. To the extent that a person maintains this illusion of invulnerability (and, to some extent, we all do in order to face possibilities of trauma in everyday life), traumatic events produce an important change in the schema: "I am not as invulnerable as I thought; this is really happening to me!"

Another schema that is challenged is the one that posits that there are reasons why traumatic events do or do not occur. This schema has to do with personal control. "Bad things don't happen to me because I protect myself by being careful or good." When people hold this belief, a traumatic event calls into question the reason for the event. Here we have the rumination about "Why did this happen to me?" If people feel that they have been living life carefully, the troubling answer might be, "Things like this can happen no matter what precautions I take." This is a shattering of the original schema, and a very different idea about personal control emerges. But if people see that they have been careless, they can maintain their original schema by engaging in behavioral self-blame: "I should have been more careful, and I will be in the future." A similar set of outcomes can be seen when people use the assumption that by being good, they will be invulnerable to trauma. When a traumatic event occurs, they may assume either that "Bad things can happen to good people," producing a profound change in their schema, or that "I've been bad, and this is my punishment." This may be a profound change as well, depending on how central this view of self as worthy might be (McCann & Pearlman, 1990).

Events are traumatic to the extent that they challenge higher-order schemas that are related to comprehensibility, meaningfulness, and manageability. But growth is possible only because of change in schemas; we propose that growth *is* change in schemas. For example, people who experience an illness and think, "I always thought this could happen to me someday," may be able to get on with managing the problem rather than ruminating about issues of comprehensibility. If they manage it better than they thought they could, this could influence the self-schema, leading to a greater sense of confidence and mastery, that is, growth. However, if they manage it well, but had predicted that they could, there will be a positive outcome in terms of successful coping, but none of the changes in worldview that we are describing. But if this process is seen as particularly meaningful, a schematic change and growth could occur. For example, an unsurprising trauma and successful coping might allow others to derive some inspiration, giving the whole process some meaning. Consider what professional golfer Paul Azinger said about his battle with lymphoma:

> This whole ordeal, this has been one of the greatest experiences of my life. I can honestly say that. One of the best things about it is that it's given me [a] forum to encourage and inspire a lot of people. It's taught me a lot. (Dorman, 1994)[1]

Principle 2: Certain Assumptions Are More Resistant to Disconfirmation by Any Events, and Therefore Reduce Possibilities for Schema Change and Growth

To the degree that a person's assumptions allow some flexibility or absorption of shock from trauma, suffering can be mitigated. In this way, traumatic events lose their sting, and growth is less likely because existing schemas are unchanged. The individual's experience may be one of strengthening previously held beliefs. These beliefs have served the function of ameliorating emotional distress and controlling rumination. Religious schemas are included in this category. These higher-order beliefs are not open to empirical disconfirmation because they can account for virtually any events, and they allow for comprehensibility and meaning to survive the experience with trauma. However, some people do seem to go through a spiritual reappraisal, finally coming to the conclusion that their original beliefs were shallow or incomplete (Schwartzberg & Janoff-Bulman, 1991; Stutts, Calhoun, Tedeschi, & Cann, 1994) or that their existing beliefs are stronger or more fully developed. The changes in the content of these beliefs or the willingness to rely on them represents a schematic change.

Principle 3: The Reconstrual After Trauma Must Include Some Positive Evaluation for Growth to Occur

There are various combinations of evaluations that may result from the personal struggle with trauma. Both self and world may be seen more negatively—perhaps a mean place where an insignificant self is victimized. Or, the world may be seen positively and the self negatively—a challenging, potentially rewarding environment of which the self has been unable to take advantage. Or, the self may be viewed positively and the world negatively—an unpredictable, often threatening environment with which the self copes in heroic fashion. Or, the world and self both may be viewed positively—a challenging, potentially rewarding environment with which the self copes in heroic fashion. Meaningfulness, comprehensibility, and manageability are maximized in the latter combination of valences. They are minimized in the first.

For growth to occur, there must be some positive evaluation, and this must include some positive change in self. This is often revealed by successful attempts at managing the trauma. However, even when primary control strategies fail, the use of secondary control, and the acceptance that some goals must be put aside, can be experienced as success because of the emotional relief that comes with putting aside the struggle. Seeing oneself as "wise enough to know the difference" between what one can change and what one cannot, in the words of the serenity prayer, can be viewed as a positive change in self-schema. Secondary control has important implications for saving the individual from continuing failure and frustration, and the development of an extreme external, passive attitude that undercuts most useful action. More active coping attempts are associated with assumptions that life is controllable and that one is powerful, at least over events relevant to this trauma. But these active strategies must be directed toward events that indeed are likely to respond to inputs.

Principle 4: Different Types of Events Are
Likely to Produce Different Types of Growth

One general distinction among traumatic events, or those that have the potential to be traumatic, has to deal with causal attributions. Events can be seen to have resulted from actions of self, others, or chance. When events are perceived to have been brought on by one's own acts (e.g., the carelessness or badness referred to above), the potential for growth lies in changes in self-schema. The self may need to be transformed into something more aware or righteous.

When traumatic events are attributed to the actions of others, schematic change may involve accounting for these betrayals or victimizations. Although blaming others may make growth less likely (Tennen & Affleck, 1990), growth may occur when a person is able to better assess others' motives and develop strategies to avoid being hurt again. Rather than a general mistrust being produced, the enhanced capabilities for making interpersonal judgments can produce more freedom to act in a trusting fashion.

When events are seen as due to chance, there can be a reappraisal of personal choices that can affect these apparently random events. Few events are ever perceived to be truly due to chance. Illnesses are often related to lifestyle choices. Certain disasters are more likely in certain locations (e.g., floods on the coast, toxic releases near a chemical factory), and people may reconsider their choices to live in certain places or engage in certain activities. Through this process, life priorities may be reconsidered.

But different types of events are related to different growth outcomes, less because of the characteristics of the event or attributions made about it, and more because of the response made by oneself and others after the occurrence of the event. After all, growth occurs after the event and through the process of trying to manage it and find meaning in it, rather than only understanding its occurrence. Events that lead to help being offered within a collaborative framework may produce the most growth. For example, cardiac rehabilitation patients whose spouses provided assistance while discouraging dependence and passivity have had better recoveries (Gorkin, Follick, Wilkin, & Niaura, 1994). Such collaboration may increase a sense that a traumatic event can be managed and may also demonstrate that others can be relied on, changing schemas about others in a positive way.

Finding that one can use the traumatic event and/or the recovery from it to help others is also a powerful route to managing it and finding meaning in it. This is one of the benefits often cited for mutual help support groups. To find that one still has something to offer others after having been in a trauma can be an impressive demonstration of personal strength and worth, producing change in self-schema. For example, Norris, Riad, and Kaniasty (1993) found that the more support received and given to others following Hurricanes Hugo and Andrew, the greater the positive affect and self-esteem. Certain kinds of traumas, by which many people are affected, seem to provide more opportunities for this kind of reciprocal support. In situations in which traumas are experienced in isolation, mutual support groups create opportunities to exchange support with others.

Individuals appraise events as traumatic in relation to their perceived personal resources. When events are not challenging enough, they are not likely to change schemas or provoke a serious reconsideration of them. Events that overwhelm personal resources may produce negative outcomes, as discussed in Chapter 2. But when personal resources and schemas are seriously challenged, growth becomes possible. Emotionally significant schemas, those that reflect central needs prior to the traumatic event (McCann & Pearlman, 1990), are often most challenged by highly traumatic events, and growth is most likely when these most important schemas undergo revision. For example, rape may challenge the schema involving trust or benevolence, and a reconsideration of this may promote a more healthy way of choosing relationships in the future (Burt & Katz, 1987; Veronen & Kilpatrick, 1983).

Principle 5: Personality
Characteristics Are Related to Possibility for Growth

Certain personality characteristics are related to the tendency for the survivor to perceive growth as having occurred as the result of trauma, as discussed in Chapter 4. This may be because some persons cope with trauma in a way that leads to growth, or because they are more able to see the silver lining, or both. Self-efficacy, locus of control, hardiness, optimism, and related constructs have been implicated in successful coping. These elements of creativity (Strickland, 1989) allow a letting go of conventional approaches to problems, are associated with a tendency to act upon the environment, and produce an ability to bring order out of chaos. As we discussed before, an alertness to the environment and flexibility allow people to creatively construe their world to enhance comprehensibility, make plans, and act within limits that allow the situation to be manageable.

Principle 6: Growth Occurs When the Trauma Assumes a Central Place in the Life Story

As a result of the flexing of the schemas, system of constructs, assumptive world, and so on, the self, the world, and the traumatic event itself take on a different character, one that has a "place" in the story of one's life (Thompson & Janigian, 1988). Only in hindsight, as the effects of this event are not just seen but constructed (Howard, 1989; Kelly, 1955; McAdams, 1993; van den Broek & Thurlow, 1991), will the trauma carry meaning. In the context of the life narrative, it becomes comprehensible, and self and world become comprehensible again as well.

The central role of a traumatic event is often found in the references people make to life "before" and "after" this watershed event. These references are usually accompanied by statements about their naiveté or incomplete understanding of things before the trauma and what they have now come to realize about themselves, others, and events in life. They now *comprehend*, or can *manage* what they didn't know they could, or find life to have a *meaning* for them that it never had before the trauma. The sense is that the story of one's life took a sharp turn, and it was a turn for the better, as Jerry stated in the first chapter. There is some indication that people's perceptions of improvements in self may be an outgrowth of implicit theories of stability and change (Ross, 1989). Given that cultures contain the idea that suffering produces transformations, as discussed in Chapter 1, people may be prone to look for such transformations following traumatic events.

For many survivors, the struggle with trauma represents the first time they have considered their life as a "story," or having some theme or pattern. Before the trauma, they may have been simply living it out without giving it much thought. The trauma stopped them in their tracks and produced a more conscious consideration of their choices, capabilities, and the point of it all, and it becomes a key element in the current life story (Shelton, Calhoun, & Tedeschi, 1994). This narrative may then serve as a "generativity script" (McAdams, 1989). This is a plan for what can be done during the rest of life in order to leave a legacy. A clear sense of this plan gives future choices and the events of the past, including the trauma, a purpose or meaning. Now the entire life can be seen in the context of this plan to leave something important for others.

Principle 7: Wisdom Is a Product of Growth

It appears that the growth that is perceived by those experiencing traumatic events produces a kind of thinking and perspective that is similar to what is described by those who are building models of wisdom. Baltes and Smith (1990), for example, describe wisdom as knowledge that allows people to succeed in the fundamental life tasks of life planning, life review, and life management. Wisdom is involved with the "fundamental pragmatics of life." This life interpretation and management includes "knowledge about one's self and one's own life biography and goals" (Baltes & Smith, 1990, p. 96). According to these researchers, practice with problems of life, personal efficacy, and cognitive mechanics are among the antecedents of wisdom.

A common element in the positive changes wrought by traumatic events is an appreciation of paradox. Of course, the fundamental paradox here is that good can come from bad or that loss can produce gain. But there are other specific paradoxes as well. One is that one must do and not do. Taking action is necessary to manage difficulties, but the tolerance of inaction, waiting, and accepting is also important. Another paradox is that one must learn to rely on others, but also that, ultimately, managing a crisis is up to the individual. Another paradox is that the trauma is in the past and one must learn how to keep it there; on the other hand, it is more easily resolved if it is integrated into present life in some constructive fashion. These paradoxical themes are woven into the reports of growth heard from people who experience trauma and represent to them the wisdom of life to which they have become privy.

This logic, based on contradiction and paradox (i.e., dialectical thinking), has been described as the cognitive component of wisdom, which is integrated with an affective component (Kramer, 1990). Wisdom has been described as a dialectic "bounded by the transcendence of limitations and . . . by their acceptance . . . tested by circumstances in which we have to decide what is changeable and what is not" (Birren & Fisher, 1990, p. 324). Wisdom can function to resolve life dilemmas, engage in life review, and develop spiritually. It facilitates these functions through relativistic and dialectical thinking that permits "the recognition of individuality, context, possibilities for change and growth, and both cognition and affect and by allowing for effective interpersonal skills" (Kramer, 1990, p. 305). Wise people are also characterized by their serenity, indicating that they manage emotional distress efficiently. For people who achieve this kind of knowledge, it does not seem paradoxical at all but, instead, integrative. This perspective cannot be appreciated purely through the intellect because wisdom "is knowledge of the world gained through experience of the world rather than through the prism of our intellectual conception of the world" (Osborne & Baldwin, 1982, p. 272). Traumatic events are particularly powerful sources of this experientially based knowledge and contribute to knowing that wisdom has a strong affective element in addition to the cognitive one.

Summary of Principles of Growth

In sum, psychological growth is perceived when (a) some change has taken place in the view of self and/or world; (b) this change is perceived to have resulted in a more profound understanding of the self and world; (c) this understanding allows for changes in behavior that are seen to be effective in warding off future distress, engaging in activities previously unconsidered or untried, or providing rewards previously unattained; (d) what is lost is devalued or transformed into a more valuable present and future; and (e) the changes that occurred appear to be possible because of the struggle with the challenges presented by trauma, and perhaps *only* because of the trauma. As a result, survivors of trauma perceive themselves as wiser and blessed, although this is paradoxically the result of loss or suffering.

A General Model for Personal Growth Resulting From Trauma

We contend that the process of responding to traumatic life events, and the effects of these events on the individual, can best be understood as part of a self-regulatory system of feedback loops. Many psychologists have viewed person-environmental and intrapersonal interactions this way, and have taken pains to emphasize the active, creative nature of the individual in appraising the environment, his or her own behavior, and its consequences (Bandura, 1978; Carver & Scheier, 1981; Hamilton et al., 1993). Feedback systems are also features of Schaefer and Moos's (1992) model of personal growth. Although this introduces some complexity into the explanation, we believe that it is the only way to make sense out of the phenomenon of perceiving benefits in situations that are clearly dreaded, avoided, and distressing.

Our model for the process whereby growth occurs following traumatic events is presented in schematic form in Figure 6.1. Each number, 1 through 7, refers to a large panel that contains several related major elements of the model. Arrows indicate important effects. Panels 3, 6, and 7 are divided into emotional, cognitive, and behavioral elements. We will briefly review this model, which incorporates the previously discussed elements involved in the process by which survivors perceive personal growth as resulting from trauma.

Personality characteristics (Panel 1), discussed in detail in Chapter 4, are involved in the initial responses to trauma and throughout the process of responding to trauma and growing from it. These characteristics can also be changed somewhat by the experience, and this personality development is an aspect of the growth that people perceive. We summarize the characteristics of people predisposed to growth as the creative sort described by Strickland (1989): able to let go of conventional approaches to problems and reconstrue their situation; able to bring order out of chaos; and having a tendency to act upon their environment while regulating behavior within limits.

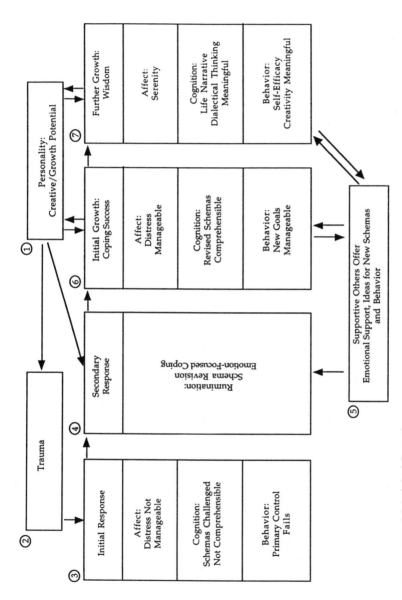

Figure 6.1. A Model of Growth

89

However, people whose personality development is maximized by the struggle with adversity also have room to grow (i.e., their creativity is in an embryonic stage).

The trauma itself (Panel 2) is initially appraised according to the personality tendencies of the person involved. People who are more optimistic, hardy, internally controlled, and efficacious may first have a sense that they can cope successfully, usually through primary control strategies, with whatever has happened. But to some extent, any trauma that results in growth must hinder these usual ways of operating (Panel 3). After initial shock or denial, this produces significant emotional distress, a serious challenge to higher-order schemas, and a failure of primary control strategies (i.e., those behaviors that are attempts to reverse or halt the effects of the trauma). As a result, the situation is deemed to be unmanageable, incomprehensible, or unmeaningful. This sets in motion the "Secondary Response" characterized by the rumination represented in Panel 4. Rumination leads to schema revision and attempts to relieve distress through emotion-focused coping strategies, and these are affected by the personality characteristics of the traumatized person.

Panel 5 represents the influences of other people who may come to the aid of the person. They may offer emotional support, new ways to understand what has happened, and ways of behaving that might make the situation more manageable. This support continues as the traumatized person proceeds to the next phase of this process but allows the person to find a unique way to handle the situation.

Panel 6, "Initial Growth," represents the influence of support from others, of personality characteristics, and of schema revision that has taken place on the acceptance of the unchangeable aspects of the situation, the setting of new goals that are more realistic, and the development of a new understanding of what has happened. This is successful coping, where the situation is understood, emotional distress decreases, and action is taken to successfully obtain revised goals. The person also finds that personal resources are sufficient to be able to assist others. As a result of this process, the situation is perceived to be more manageable and comprehensible, and some initial growth is possible. Growth in this case takes the form of a sense of personal strength, a recognition that others can be helpful in ways not previously experienced, and an understanding of the vicissitudes of life. The degree of growth in turn contributes to positive change in the personality.

In Panel 7, more growth occurs after additional cognitive processing by a particularly creative personality. This rumination is a somewhat more reflective, expansive version because the situation has become manageable and comprehensible, and there is less emotional distress. The personality development that initially took place (Panel 6) can be a springboard to the growth of Panel 7. This growth is the wisdom to which we previously referred. There is emotional serenity together with an acute appreciation for life and an exhilaration that can come from a recognition that the self is vulnerable yet strong. Cognitive changes are characterized by a review and revision of the life narrative, and development of dialectical thinking that allows for an appreciation of the paradoxes and contradictions that have been involved in this difficult path through trauma and its aftermath (Schwartzberg, 1993). This leads to new creativity in behavior that is reflected in enhanced personal relationships, which are deepened because of lessons in empathy and the experience of support and caring. The traumatic experience becomes most meaningful, from the perspective of the person who has experienced it, when this wisdom has developed. There is likely a reciprocal relationship between wisdom and meaningfulness as well. The meaningfulness of life is deepened when the preciousness of what remains is enhanced by the losses.

Note

1. Copyright © 1994 by The New York Times Company. Reprinted by permission.

SUPPORT AND INTERVENTION

I'm going to spend whatever time I have left trying to give some hope to others.[1]

—Jim Valvano, dying of cancer

An element in recovery from traumatic events is the social support system to which people have access. The effect of this support depends on what is necessary given the circumstances of the event, the resources of the person needing help, and how the support is offered (Barrera, 1988; Cutrona, 1990; Dakof & Taylor, 1990; Hobfoll & Vaux, 1993). Social support may have beneficial effects through the operation of many different processes (Ell & Dunkel-Schetter, 1994). In this chapter, we will not attempt to review the voluminous literature on social support and coping, nor to offer a complete model of how to provide crisis intervention, therapy for trauma victims, or reverse symptoms of posttraumatic stress disorder. For extensive descriptions of psychotherapy with traumatized people, the reader is encouraged to consult the excellent sources that are available (Everstine & Everstine, 1993; Herman, 1992; Horowitz, 1986; McCann & Pearlman, 1990; Monahon, 1993; Ochberg, 1988; Saigh, 1992; van der Kolk, 1986; Wilson, 1989). Instead, we will draw on the literature on social support and intervention to suggest how supportive others—in the form of friends and family, other traumatized people, and professionals—can encourage growth in people who have experienced trauma. Because there is virtually no mention in the literature of what might promote psychological growth, we will extrapolate from what is available. We will be using our model of growth presented in Chapter 6 as a guide to the tasks that confront people in the aftermath of trauma to determine what assistance might be useful in accomplishing these tasks in a manner that can lead to psychological growth. We will focus on general principles of constructive interaction with the traumatized person that can produce growth.

The focus will be on three broad sources of support that may be available to people coping with the aftermath of trauma: the existing social network, other people who have experienced similar traumas, and professionals. As shown in Chapter 6 (Figure 6.1, Panel 5), supportive others can have an impact during the process of rumination, on promoting initial coping success and growth, and during the phase of additional growth that may be possible. Each kind of supportive other may have a specialized role in these processes. Intimates who are friends or family members may provide all the emotional support necessary. A larger system may be helpful in instrumental tasks such as gathering information about the difficulties encountered and how to cope (Hobfoll et al., 1991). Professionals such as clergy, primary care physicians, and, more rarely, counselors and psychotherapists may be consulted for more specialized information or if the informal networks are not sufficient. Professional sources of support are most effective in producing positive outcomes when they are integrated with the informal network (Schaefer & Moos, 1992).

The Role of Friends and Family

In general, the quality of the relationships with family and friends before and after the traumatic event plays a role in determining the likelihood for growth. If good relationships can be maintained or improved, growth may be possible. For example, there is a substantial literature that indicates that among cardiac patients, long-term quality of a marriage, particularly emotional support reflected in the degree of intimacy and stress, predicts recovery and quality of life years after cardiac events (Helgeson, 1991; Kulik & Mahler, 1993;

Waltz, 1986; Waltz & Bandura, 1988). Similar effects have been reported among families experiencing economic deprivation, with the hardships strengthening father-child relationships when marriages were strong (Elder, 1979). On the other hand, poorly functioning marriages appear to produce additional stress because of lack of communication and understanding (Coyne, Wortman, & Lehman, 1988). It is probably unrealistic to expect that such marriages will benefit from the substantial stress of a traumatic event. Whether coping is unsuccessful or psychological growth is experienced, it may be useful to consider the process of coping as embedded within the family context rather than simply the task of the individual directly affected by a traumatic event (Coyne & Smith, 1994).

Of the three categories of social support mentioned here, friends and family are likely to be the only supportive others who have had an ongoing relationship with the person prior to the trauma. Therefore, they have already played a role in preparing this person to cope with it. Werner (1984) has specific recommendations for promoting resiliency in children that focus on the actions of supportive others *prior* to traumatic events:

1. Accept temperamental idiosyncrasies and allow some experiences that challenge, but do not overwhelm, coping abilities
2. Convey a sense of responsibility and caring, and reward helpfulness and cooperation
3. Encourage activities that can serve as a source of gratification and self-esteem
4. Model a conviction that life makes sense despite the inevitable adversities, as well as a faith that "things will work out" and that odds can be overcome
5. Encourage reaching out to others and carrying out some socially desirable task to alleviate others' distress

Although these suggestions were meant to foster resilience in vulnerable children, they may also be important for supportive family and friends to keep in mind after trauma strikes. It also appears important that family and friends support in a way that balances clear displays of caring and willingness to take on tasks that the person cannot manage with encouragement to self-manage as much as possible.

For example, oversolicitousness by anxious family members is often a source of conflict for cardiac rehabilitation patients (Jenkins, Stanton, Savageau, Delinger, & Klein, 1983). Supportive others must allow for recovery and possible growth despite their own anxieties regarding the path the person is taking, just as parents must guard against overprotectiveness so that children can develop their strengths. Because family and friends, as well as the person experiencing the trauma, may have little or no information about or experience with such an event and its aftermath, it might be difficult for them to determine what appropriate support might be. In these situations, professional guidance as an alternative to informal support can be useful (Kahana & Kinney, 1991). What is appropriate also changes over time as the person needing support regains emotional and, in cases of accidents and injuries, physical strength and capabilities.

Family members share schemas to some extent (Constantine, 1986; Reiss, 1981). A common appraisal of the causes of the trauma and how to cope with it may be important in the development of a mutuality between the trauma survivor and supportive family in facing the aftermath of trauma. There is some indication that lack of understanding or acceptance of a spouse's perspective on a trauma may lead to additional survivor stress and difficulty with recovery. On the other hand, as married couples cope together with trauma, the development of a shared understanding of the situation can lead to positive effects on the marital relationship (Patterson, 1989). Despite the evidence that support may evaporate when a person experiences traumatic events (Barrera, 1988; Silver & Urbanowicz, 1990), in some cases experiencing the trauma reveals the depth of caring from others (Zemore & Shepel, 1989). The recognition of this benefit may introduce the idea that additional benefits may be possible as a result of the situation, promoting the process of growth.

Because of the very nature of the relationships, the well-being of close friends and family can be negatively affected, in many of the same ways as the people who directly experience the loss, by the distressing things that happen to the person who is directly challenged by the trauma (Coyne, Ellard, & Smith, 1990). Friends and family may protect themselves by either trying to minimize the situation of the traumatized person or trying to improve their situation. Failure in these attempts may produce depression and withdrawal of support by friends and family (Gottlieb & Wagner, 1991). In contrast, when supportive listening, empathy, and encouragement are offered, both the helper and the person needing support feel better (Notarius & Herrick, 1988).

Providing support to a family member or friend who has been traumatized can be emotionally and physically draining. The good news, however, is that many of the benefits we identified as resulting from coping directly with a major difficulty can occur for caregivers as well. For example, parents of children who are handicapped, high-risk, or diabetic (Abbott & Meredith, 1986; Affleck, Allen, et al., 1985; Affleck, Tennen, & Gershman, 1985) have reported that in their struggle with the challenges presented by their caregiving role, they experienced many of the same benefits reported by people directly affected by trauma.

Mutual Help

Although clinicians can assist in many ways, similar others often are more credible and are preferred over therapists with no personal experience with the difficulty in question (Tedeschi & Calhoun, 1993). For example, individuals who have lost a loved one to suicide express an unambiguous preference for support from others who have lost a loved one in a similar way. They report that these interactions are more helpful to them than interactions with people bereaved for other reasons (Wagner & Calhoun, 1991). Similar preferences are expressed by people faced with serious illnesses (Shontz, 1975), by combat veterans (Shay, 1994), and by bereaved parents (Tedeschi & Calhoun, 1993). Because of these preferences, many localities have a variety of support groups providing this often-preferred assistance for people who have experienced similar life problems (Wortman & Lehman, 1985).

There may be unique opportunities for personal growth when there is contact with people who have experienced a similar fate (Lehman, Ellard, & Wortman, 1986). Although it is useful for supportive others to communicate that felt distress is normal and that it will not always be so intense (Selby & Calhoun, 1980), it is especially helpful if this is said by a person who has experienced a similar crisis. Such a person provides a very powerful model of the possibilities that exist (Helgeson & Taylor, 1993). This is true if the helper is not perceived as inordinately superior to the person, leading the person to discount the degree to which the model was once in a similar circumstance, with similar personal characteristics and resources (Bandura, 1977). Helpers offer reassurance about the nature of the present distress, and a way to reconceptualize present experience and what the future may hold. This relieves some of the distress and provides hope for the future.

People who have experienced similar difficulties often provide a useful way of understanding the coping process because they may be able to discuss specific emotional reactions and concerns that victims experience. They provide a positive view of circumstances that victims can use in attempting to cope. For example, in one of our studies (Tedeschi & Calhoun, 1988), a man confined to a wheelchair reported that he had heard another person in a similar situation describe his limitations in an eye-opening fashion: "Before I was disabled, there were 10,000 things I could do in life. Now there are only 2000. But you only get a chance to do 150 to 200 anyway, so I'm going to make the most of them." Such interpretations are most powerful for a person when they come from credible sources; otherwise, they could be construed as platitudes (Affleck, Tennen, & Gershman, 1985).

People who have coped successfully are highly credible sources to those in distress who have little idea how to proceed in coping with a novel and frightening situation (Wagner & Calhoun, 1991). For this reason, mutual support groups are often a powerful tool in aiding even those who appear to have otherwise adequate support systems. Those who have confronted similar circumstances can provide a springboard to capable coping and ultimately to perceiving benefits from the crisis. These veterans of trauma accomplish this by offering reassurance about the normality of emotional distress, modeling specific understandings and actions that can be used to cope, and providing evidence that the crisis can be managed.

Mutual support groups may be particularly helpful in encouraging the search for benefits because individuals may actually *observe these positive changes in others* before they begin to experience them themselves. This is why it is useful in such support groups to include people who are veterans of the struggle with the crisis as well as those who are relatively new to the crisis. This inclusion may be most useful when the veterans demonstrate that they are a bit farther on the road to successful coping and that they are similar in ways that are important to the more recently affected individual. In support groups for bereaved parents, for example, members often request, especially at the start, to have former group members return to tell them of their experiences and how they are managing now. These people provide clear hope to the bereaved parents, who at the beginning have no idea how they will manage to survive their grief, let alone benefit from their pain. The veteran group members remain a source of inspiration and represent the possibility of a future to these struggling parents.

Mutual support groups also provide a unique opportunity to be helpful to others, maintaining a sense of mutuality and reciprocity (Antonucci & Jackson, 1990). These altruistic acts have been viewed as productive, mature responses to trauma (Vaillant, 1977), and *giving support* is equally helpful, according to reports of support group members (Taylor, Falke, Mazel, & Hilsberg, 1988). Self-esteem may be bolstered by the experience of being helpful, and there may be the thought that because of the unusual knowledge gained by the experience of the trauma, the person is in a remarkable position to be helpful to others.

When survivors experience the satisfaction of helping others, and do not stigmatize those they help, they are more willing to seek help themselves without feeling stigmatized (Hobfoll et al., 1991). Helping others can also produce a greater sense of intimacy with others in similar circumstances, especially because the issues addressed are so personal and emotional. The recognition that one has something precious to offer other people in great turmoil can produce a sense that one now has a gift: intimate knowledge of the traumatic experience and an ability to empathize with similar others in a way few could. There may develop a sense of belonging, paid for dearly, and therefore very valuable.

The growth that occurs when one is seen as part of a community of people similarly traumatized seems to be the *initial* growth mentioned in Chapter 6 (Figure 6.1, Panel 6). But moving on from this to *additional* growth requires a recognition of separateness from others in similar positions. "Major recovery, however, requires that personal narrative be particular, not general" (Shay, 1994, p. 192). The events and the personal struggle are seen in terms of a unique experience. This makes necessary additional rumination and a more profound exploration of existential issues of aloneness. Even when support comes in a group setting, the experience is personal because an important experience in small groups is the storytelling that occurs. By telling about their own histories, people create meaningful life stories. Repetition of stories and the interpretations of others can expose the layers of meaning in them, provide new insights, and produce a better understanding of the past and a new direction for the future (Wuthnow, 1994).

But even the unique story of an individual is elevated when a universal theme is discovered. Particularly relevant to our discussion is an example cited by Wuthnow of the apparently miraculous delivery of healthy twins after a difficult pregnancy by a mother who was a member of a church group. "[The group] often told the whole story again, noting that God does not take away people's problems but sustains people in hard times and helps them to grow in the process" (Wuthnow, 1994, p. 298).

Professional Help

People facing traumatic events sometimes find benefits because the event puts them into contact with professional helpers whom they would not otherwise have met. Professional helpers can have a powerful effect on survivors' perceptions of themselves, their values, and their goals in life because they become aware of general life issues beyond the traumatic event itself that may need to be addressed to speed recovery. For example, Veronen and Kilpatrick (1983) describe rape victims whose lives changed substantially for the better after being treated at rape crisis centers by professionals who emphasized the recognition of how clients might have allowed themselves to be victimized in other ways. Inmates in prisons are sometimes rehabilitated through the influence of people who provide literacy, relationship, or job skills, without which inmates would be likely to pursue criminality as their only apparent option. To a large extent, these opportunities are serendipitous, according to where a person may be treated or which support professional makes contact with the person. This "agency-mediated change" (Veronen & Kilpatrick, 1983) may be crucial to beginning the process of finding benefit in crisis for many people.

SUPPORTING SELF-PERCEPTIONS
OF BENEFITS AND GROWTH

One of the central goals of psychotherapy and counseling is to assist individuals in liberating themselves by searching for, finding, and acknowledging the truth. Illusions and distortions of reality are regarded as inconsistent with the full functioning of human beings (Colvin & Block, 1994). It has also been suggested that clinicians who work with people who have suffered major stressful events may need to develop a greater tolerance for the therapeutic utility of illusions (Taylor & Brown, 1988). The self-perceptions of benefit or growth that we have discussed will be judged by some researchers and clinicians to be illusory, but such perceptions of growth arising from negative events can assist the client in maintaining self-esteem, enhancing the sense of control, and keeping hope alive when despair is an ever-present threat. These outcomes, in turn, can foster improvements in mental well-being and physical health (Taylor, 1990). Clinicians need to develop an increased tolerance for the individual's tendency to perceive benefit in suffering, even if from the clinician's point of view this involves a certain degree of illusion.

Much of what we have discussed in this book involves the interpretation, the narrative account, that individuals make of their encounter with tragedies in life. Whereas some of the benefits we have discussed may be reflected in "objective" measures, many more of these involve the way in which sense is made out of what happened. So when an individual sees what he or she believes to be a benefit arising from misfortune, professionals committed to "the truth" should guard against the temptation of robbing that individual of the freedom to view life's events from his or her own perspective. This has been described as "imposed suffering," where clinicians "observe that people whom they regard as unfortunate are, in fact, happy and well-adjusted . . . indicating the operation of repression or denial" (Shontz, 1975, p. 93). We have never encountered a client in our practice, nor a case in the literature, where a client was hurt when the clinician respected the client's own interpretation of good coming from negative events. On the other hand, clinicians who, in the name of "truth" or "insight," rob clients of their own understanding of good coming from the struggle with negative events increase the chances of harming individuals psychologically.

Clinicians and supportive others should also recognize that the growth experienced by the client may be difficult to appreciate or grasp by people who are only observers and were not directly affected by a traumatic event, and that in some ways the person who experienced the trauma may eventually surpass the clinician in wisdom. On the other hand, clinicians who are most effective are emotionally and experientially engaged in the process of healing that traumatized people go through, producing a growth in personal consciousness in both the client and clinician (Osborne & Baldwin, 1982).

RESPECTFUL INTERVENTION

Although it is an admirable goal to help clients increase the benefits they perceive from dealing with trauma, *is it possible to do so?* The literature clearly indicates that individuals will perceive benefits, but the available information is unclear about the influence that professionals, other traumatized people, and various forms of social support may have in the development of these benefits. The amount of change and improvement that can occur for clients in psychotherapy is limited (Costa & McCrae, 1986; Mahoney, 1991), and that limitation seems likely in this context as well. However, there are avenues open to the clinician that can be pursued when working with people who confront life trauma. The clinician collaborates with the client on developing a narrative reconstruction of events that is coherent and allows understanding of what has occurred (Russell & van den Broek, 1992; Thompson & Janigian, 1988).

Pathways to providing support and intervention with people confronting traumatic events will become more clear if one remembers that these individuals are confronting the tasks of managing the emotional and situational sequelae, understanding what has happened and the consequences, and finding some meaning in it. These tasks are complicated if the circumstances are continuing to change or if outcomes are still unclear (e.g., an illness that is progressing rapidly). But if the trauma is essentially finished or the consequences are clear (e.g., an illness is clearly terminal), then the process of managing, comprehending, and finding meaning can proceed without constant readjustment to changing circumstances.

Generally, when providing support to people who have experienced trauma, it is crucial to *be respectful of their individual process of coping*. Most of us share some general ideas about how people should react to difficulties and how long we believe people should feel poorly about their losses in life (Wortman & Silver, 1989). When people in crisis do not respond the way we believe they should, we may be less inclined to want to help them. This can create difficulties because assumptions about how people ought to react and about how "most people" react may be wrong. For example, in the recent past, clinicians described a particular time frame for the duration of grief—the assumption was that grief should be over in 1 or 2 years. Now, however, there is research that suggests that for some people, grief may last years and that this is not necessarily a sign of psychological problems. Although it is not a direct way of assisting, accepting the individual differences in reacting to trauma is an indirect way of being helpful. We take the perspective that we cannot do the work for the person. If there is a possibility for positive outcomes and further growth, it will be necessary to respect the person's way of construing, the narrative they create, their spiritual insights and development, and the pace at which they address these issues.

It is important to recognize which task a person finds most crucial at the moment. Figure 6.1 provides some guidance about this. Finding meaning is unlikely to be a top priority while things remain unmanageable and incomprehensible. (This is not to say that people are not attempting to accomplish more than one task at a time.) At the outset, being "merely" supportive is often the best approach. Being a good listener to the person facing the crisis can be a highly useful contribution to that person (Dakof & Taylor, 1990). It is best to *focus on listening without trying to solve anything* for the person in crisis. Sometimes individuals believe that to be useful, they must try to provide expertise or at least suggestions on what to do. A physical presence, accompanied by simple acceptance of what the other person is saying, is enough. Appropriate expressions of caring, affection, and concern can also be helpful. The specific words that are said are much less important than the message conveyed by attempts to understand and express caring for the other person.

IS THE CLIENT READY FOR GROWTH?

Clinicians should recognize that *timing* is an important element in the likelihood that assistance in recognizing benefits will be accepted by clients. *Immediately after a trauma has occurred is not a good time to be considering the possibility of benefit.* In this way, the traditional notion of "working through" is useful to remember, and Figure 6.1 in Chapter 6 shows which tasks are involved in this process. It appears that many people have to immerse themselves in highly negative experiences and emotions, ruminate about them, struggle through them, and finally come to some recognition of benefit after there has been time to reflect. The amount of time necessary for this is dependent on the event as well. Certain events that have provoked a great deal of guilt, anger, and irreversible loss appear to make it difficult to perceive any positives. Losing a child, for example, creates such a void in parents' lives that it may become difficult to perceive benefits. This, of course, is a matter of degree. It may be possible for a bereaved parent to say, "My family has become closer because of this," but it would be impossible to conclude, as did Jerry, the paralyzed man in Chapter 1, "It's a good thing this happened to me." A person losing a job may find that this loss forced a reconsideration of career and led to more fulfilling work and gratefulness for this job loss. But the death of a loved one may make it impossible to take the most extreme position of being grateful that the trauma occurred. Still, other benefits may be perceived.

Clinicians who are wondering whether a survivor may be able to perceive benefits should also consider *the individual's propensity for using such approaches to understanding and coping.* Questions about the way a person has handled other negative events may reveal the degree to which he or she is likely to be resilient and to perceive benefits. Clinicians can address the question of perceived benefits by asking, "Some people report that as a result of struggling with a life crisis, they have recognized some benefit of this experience for them. Has anything like this happened to you?" Even though someone may not answer in the affirmative at one point in time does not mean that perception of benefits will never occur. It will probably take longer for people who have never operated this way in the past, who are earlier in the process of recovery from trauma, who judge perception of benefit to be a betrayal, and who have had little contact with "veterans" of such events who can give permission to view coping in more positive ways.

Another way to be of help is by *striking a balance between accepting what is a normal response of pain and distress*, which may last a long time, and *not passively acquiescing and abandoning hope* that a negative outcome can be changed (Tait & Silver, 1989). There is, of course, no simple formula to decide when we should accept what the other person cannot change. But the clinician needs to keep in mind the need to try to find a compromise between what must be and what can be. When that compromise is found, the clinician may then be able to gently nudge the person in crisis in the appropriate direction of acceptance of what must be, on the one hand, and attempts to reach what can be, on the other.

A direct way of assisting the survivor of trauma in finding positive aspects in negative life events is by *reinforcing the reasonable positive interpretations* that the individual makes. This requires responding appropriately to what is initiated by the survivor, rather than offering platitudes about what wonderful opportunities tragedies really are (Tedeschi & Calhoun, 1991). The goal is not to force the individual to see things in a positive light but to listen and observe carefully and to provide support as the survivor develops positive interpretations of the difficulties experienced in the aftermath of trauma. Attempts to encourage the other person to "look on the bright side" will be unhelpful or even detrimental (Wortman & Lehman, 1985). On the other hand, it is important to avoid attempting to protect survivors from disappointment by emphasizing limits to change (Berger, 1988). Again, listening and being there are ways to be helpful. In addition, carefully attending to the small and brief indicants of positive interpretations generated by a survivor can be of help too.

The clinician can also help by *bringing into sharper focus for the client the benefits that are implicit in the context*. This can occur by either identifying possible benefits that the survivor has not yet seen or reframing the way that the person sees particular events. For example, a client once indicated that as a result of having to cope with the loss of her job and the serious illness of her husband, she had gone through a period where she almost completely lost her religious faith. The clinician, aware that the client's involvement in religious activities had increased and her faith had become more meaningful to her in recent months, indicated that "after that struggle about what you believed, your faith is now stronger than it would have been before it was tested by your troubles." The clinician's response allowed the client to identify consciously a previously unrecognized benefit of her struggle.

As with any other psychotherapeutic strategy, it is important for the clinician to time the discussion of possible benefits so that the survivor is able to consider them rather than reject them. The kinds of problems that the individual is facing will affect the ease with which the individual can see benefits. When a major loss has occurred, such as the death of a loved one, not allowing oneself to see any benefits in the struggle may be a way of being loyal to the deceased. The individual coping with such a loss may not *want* to gain from the loss of the other person. The grieving individual experiences discomfort if he or she interprets seeing benefits in the loss as a betrayal, somehow, of the other person. The clinician may need to confront this issue directly with clients. Some people may be highly reluctant to acknowledge any benefits arising from their tragedies, but the counselor may need to notice any specific benefits referred to by the client and to bring these benefits to the client's attention.

The clinician's *choice of words* in reinforcing or encouraging the perception of benefits is important. It is clearly and unambiguously important to discuss the possibility of benefits arising from the *struggle* with the trauma, and not from any loss or change that might have occurred. This attention to semantic detail is particularly important when the difficulty involves the loss of another person, pain and suffering in other people, or acts of unspeakable depravity. In choosing how to deal with the theme of perceived benefits, the clinician should carefully attend to the client's choice of words, using words and expressions that the client has already made legitimate.

USING THE SURVIVOR'S BELIEF SYSTEM

Changes in fundamental viewpoints must not begin with too much variance with the survivor's preexisting ways of understanding. New material must be assimilated into the person's "assumptive world." It may provoke additional distress when explanations are offered that undermine further the understanding a person has about his world and life, and so there must be enough newness in the message to provide additional insight or cognitive restructuring, but not so much as to further shatter all beliefs on which important life decisions have rested. There may be some assumptive worlds into which new information can be more easily assimilated. More abstract, generalized assumptions that are less directly tied to reality are more resistant to change, making adjustment less difficult (Calhoun et al., 1992; Janoff-Bulman & Timko, 1987). Martin and Tesser (1989) suggest that such efforts at assimilation constitute the experience of finding meaning described by various workers in this field (Frankl, 1963; Silver, Boon, & Stones, 1983).

As we discussed in Chapter 6, individuals with strong beliefs (e.g., "God has a plan for my life") that cannot be directly tested or disproven by empirical evidence may have a greater degree of cognitive resilience when trying to deal with the negative events that have occurred to them. In our culture, this category of assumptions and beliefs tends to be religious in nature. Although many clinicians express no discomfort with religious issues, the views that some hold of religion may make it difficult for them to seriously consider *religious beliefs* useful in dealing with trauma (Bergin, 1991; Shafranske & Malony, 1990). The available data (Pargament, 1990) suggest that religious beliefs can offer a useful avenue for coping for many individuals. To assist the survivor in coping with and growing from the trauma, clinicians must therefore become comfortable discussing religious issues.

Beliefs about the goodness and predictability of the world around us are detrimentally affected by negative events (Janoff-Bulman, 1989b). Major life trauma may increase the likelihood of distressing emotions, at least in part, because one's sense of the empirical orderliness and safety of the immediate environment is negatively affected. Religious beliefs, however, are much more resilient to challenge. The fundamental components of the systems of religious beliefs that predominate in North America (e.g., Christian and Jewish viewpoints) cannot be disconfirmed by negative events. For example, although it may be difficult for individuals to understand *why* a particular accident occurred, adherents of traditional Judeo-Christian perspectives can still regard the accident as fitting into the larger plan of a divine being. The plan may not be clear now, but as one individual put it, "When I get up there, I know it will be made clear to me."

Because many individuals report that their religious beliefs are strengthened by their struggle with adversity (Calhoun & Tedeschi,

1989-1990; Schwartzberg & Janoff-Bulman, 1991), clinicians should assist religious people as they *use their religious beliefs to assimilate life crises* into their belief systems, and as they perceive benefits (such as stronger faith) in life trauma that are mediated by religious beliefs. Because of their resilience to disconfirmation, religious beliefs offer a means for the individual to construct a meaningful understanding of what has happened. Clinicians should be aware of the utility that such metaphysical assumptions can have in assisting clients who have faced major disasters in their lives.

Metaphysical assumptions and religious beliefs can also offer a direct means for the individual to perceive benefit arising from trauma. As shown in Chapter 3, a common response of individuals who have faced major difficulties in their lives is to report that their priorities in life have changed. Many also report that their religious beliefs have been strengthened (sometimes after an initial period of doubt and searching). The crisis is often viewed as the means by which the individual was given the opportunity to change radically his or her life's path. For many people, this alteration in life priorities is viewed within a religious framework. For example, one individual said that "in a way, this was God giving me an opportunity to change my life. I know He has something important for me to do. This [serious illness] was God's way of getting the message to me that it is time to turn my life around and get started on what I have to do."

NARRATIVE DEVELOPMENT

As we discussed earlier, most people confronting highly difficult events will attempt to weave an account of the events that makes sense to them (Harvey et al., 1990; Thompson & Janigian, 1988). The client's *development of this narrative of what has happened* is a necessary basis for the client to discover meaning in the struggle with adversity. To get to any benefits or growth, the clinician must be willing to hear about all the horrific details of the trauma first. Survivors of traumas often find that other people cannot endure the telling of their whole story and the retelling of it over time that is often necessary for new perspectives to develop. A girl whose mother committed suicide described her need to tell her story, and her listeners' responses. "I had to stay with it, because it wasn't gone yet. . . . There was a certain amount of tolerance beyond which people could not deal with the magnitude of the loss that I had experienced" (Alexander, 1991, p. 16). The difficult and subtle task of the listeners to Holocaust survivors has been described as one of being unobtrusively present and attuned to the survivor's wishes for contact or to be alone, although still in the listener's presence (Auerhahn, Laub, & Peskin, 1993). By going through the journey of the trauma in a way that demonstrates a willingness to experience the distressing emotions, credibility is gained that could otherwise only be found in another survivor, if anyone. The healing power of this telling of the narrative may lie in the increased desensitization to the horror (Foa, Rothbaum, Riggs, & Murdock, 1991).

Another effect of the telling is the "communalization" of the trauma. When the listener develops empathy for the teller of the story, isolation is overcome through the sense that the listener has been enlightened by hearing this story of trauma (Shay, 1994). Perhaps then it becomes clear to the person who has suffered trauma that this is comprehensible after all, and that perhaps there could be meaning in it. If the clinician entertains any hope that the traumatized person can be positively changed by his or her struggle, the clinician must allow for a similar change in him- or herself. In listening to stories of the Holocaust, for example, clinicians confront the great existential questions and come to know themselves as well as the survivor (Auerhahn et al., 1993). Komp (1993) tells about the lessons in living that she has learned from her patients as a pediatric oncologist. Without sensitive listening, these lessons would never have been learned, and her patients also would have been deprived. Consider the response of one adolescent:

> For an agonizing hour he poured out his young-ancient soul. Then he rose from the chair with tears pouring down his face. "You're the best doctor I've ever met," he exclaimed. "No one has ever helped me as much as you have. How can I thank you?" I had never gotten to say a word to Jay. I had only listened. (p. 62)

Shay (1994) describes the same process in treating Vietnam veterans:

> To achieve trust, listeners must respect the narrator. The advice that veterans consistently give to trauma therapists is "Listen! Just listen." Respect, embodied in this kind of listening, is readiness to be changed by the narrator. The change may be small or large. It may be simply

learning something not previously known, feeling something, seeing something from a new perspective, or it may be as profound as redirection of the listener's way of being in the world. (p. 189)

There are other avenues for storytelling. Writing also may be useful in organizing traumatic events into a story that can be integrated meaningfully into one's life. There is evidence that such writing can even affect physical well-being (Pennebaker, 1990; Pennebaker, Kiecolt-Glaser, & Glaser, 1988). Mahoney (1991) and Pennebaker (1990) describe ways to direct clients in written life reviews.

For children, play therapy traditionally has been used to tell stories of events and the feelings surrounding them. With traumatized children, the therapist's role is to reengage the child's hope and help weave it into the developing story of the child's life (Monahon, 1993). The child should be helped to develop the notion that just because bad things have happened in the past, life will not be a continual repetition of loss, betrayal, or fear.

It is not easy even for a professional who is a trained and experienced listener to attend emotionally to these narratives, whether they are spoken, written, or enacted in play by a child. The professional's emotional strength must allow confrontation with what invites denial, avoidance, and judgment. The clinician must not crumble in the face of the story, but at the same time must authentically experience the emotion of the person who tells the tale (Shay, 1994). Sometimes the person suffering from trauma has survived by engaging in acts that traumatized others. In dealing with others, a clinician may not always be able to travel the relatively easy course of seeing the person they are helping as a wholly "innocent victim." People who have experienced the Holocaust, war, incest, spouse abuse, and other atrocities often have to deal with their own apparently immoral acts. Clinicians should listen with respect to people as they unfold their own accounts of their trauma, while noticing the potential for finding benefits in the struggle.

Conclusions

In sum, the clinician working with individuals who have experienced trauma cannot create positive outcomes for the survivor. But it is important that clinicians, rather than maintaining a focus on pathology, find ways to support this process of growth, even if they cannot create it. The clinician can assist the survivor in creating a narrative account of what has happened that makes sense and includes positive outcomes from the struggle. This can be done by responding to and inviting discussion about worldviews, religion, and other metaphysical beliefs. In this kind of clinical work, clinicians should regard the religious beliefs of the client as helpful in both assimilating the crisis cognitively and in opening up additional means to perceive benefits.

Clinicians can also help by encouraging interactions with other people who have suffered similar circumstances and are further along in this process, so that survivors get a peek at the positive outcomes that may be possible for them without generating a lot of resistance. The clinician can also deal with resistance by attending judiciously to appropriate context and timing, and helping the client to notice benefits that might otherwise have gone unnoticed without specifically labeling them as benefits. And when clients mention this phenomenon themselves, the clinician can be ready to support it, rather than treat such developments merely as "defenses."

Note

1. Moran, M. (1992). Copyright © 1992 by The New York Times Company. Reprinted by permission.

RESEARCH DIRECTIONS

A culturally sensitive psychology . . . is and must be based . . . [on]
what [people] say they do and what they say caused them to do what
they did.

—Jerome Bruner

This book has addressed an issue that is not new, but that only recently has received the systematic attention of investigators in the social, behavioral, and health sciences—individuals who suffer greatly often claim or demonstrate significant growth from their struggle with tragedy. We have attempted to present evidence about how common this experience is and how it happens. We have drawn on the available literature, which is still modest, and we have also drawn on our clinical experiences with people struggling to make sense out of major trauma. We have developed a general description, a model, and provided some suggestions for those attempting to assist people facing extremely difficult situations.

Many questions remain unanswered. We hope our attempt has represented a useful first step in the process of integrating what little we already know and in suggesting a framework for further work. In this chapter, we suggest questions that researchers in this area might address and briefly discuss methodological issues raised by work on growth following major trauma.

Unanswered Questions

PERSON VARIABLES

It is in the area of individual differences, perhaps, that the widest array of unanswered questions exists. *Gender* has emerged as one variable that requires further inquiry. Preliminary data have suggested that women may be more likely than men to construe benefits arising from crises. It is possible that this gender difference reflects a greater tendency on the part of women, at least in some settings, to describe positive spiritual and relationship changes emerging from the struggle with trauma (Tedeschi & Calhoun, in press). This tendency may reflect a difference in the coping strategies used by women (Bijur, Wallston, Smith, Lifrak, & Friedman, 1993), and these strategies in turn may produce a greater likelihood of psychological growth. However, there may be less empirical support for gender-specific coping strategies than has been assumed (Thoits, 1991). Although the reason for it remains unclear, we found that perceptions of growth by severely traumatized women rose twice as high as those of traumatized men, suggesting that women may be more capable than men of learning or benefiting from difficult life experiences (Tedeschi & Calhoun, in press).

The individual's *age and developmental stage* may be significantly related to the degree to which growth occurs. Erikson (1950) suggested that although wisdom tends to develop in the later stages of life as a result of integrative personality processes, such growth can also occur at earlier stages. But the degree to which psychological growth can occur may be limited by the level of cognitive development. Even so, it would be interesting to see what children and adolescents are capable of.

The psychological growth and construal of benefits arising from highly stressful life situations goes beyond the empirically established and widely accepted concept of "resilience," or the ability to bounce back from difficulties. Moving beyond successful coping to growth appears to be possible in some children and adolescents. There are reports of some children perceiving development as accruing from their life traumas. For example, a 9-year-old girl said the following about her father's death: "Now I realize that no one can last forever and I think it's made me a stronger person" (Krementz, 1983, pp.

98-99). When questioned about likely outcomes for children whose parents divorce, mid-latency children have been remarkably optimistic, seeing such events as crises that will be overcome, rather than as enduring traumas (Plunkett, Schaefer, Kalter, Okla, & Schreier, 1986). However, despite these childhood expectations, college students who have experienced divorce in their families of origin are less optimistic about their future marriages and anticipate that they would trust their spouse less (Franklin et al., 1990).

It appears that some children do achieve some growth as a result of struggles with adversity and that some do not. Pediatric cancer survivors have been judged to have improved social/peer interactions in half of the cases and poorer interactions in the other cases (Fritz, Williams, & Amylon, 1988), and the positive changes were not necessarily in those who had the easiest course. Furthermore, many changes were subtle, qualitative, but important changes: "clarified values, heightened sensitivity to others, increased altruism, and altered perceptions of the vigor and vulnerability of their own bodies that many survivors remarked upon in the interviews" (Fritz et al., 1988, pp. 560-561). Among bereaved adolescents, there have been reports of development of a "faith consciousness" and a "deepening understanding of human existence" (Balk & Hogan, in press). It appears that children beyond certain developmental levels may be capable of perceiving psychological growth in ways that are similar to adults.

It could be argued that people in late adolescence and early adulthood could be seeing themselves as undergoing rapid and significant maturation, and there is evidence that adolescents may normally be quite optimistic (Plunkett et al., 1986). Also, first experiences with life traumas might be especially significant to a developing cognitive system, producing a tendency to perceive substantial insights from coping with these crises.

Closely related to the issue of developmental stage and possibilities for growth is the importance of looking at personal growth using longitudinal methodologies. What is the temporal process involved in growth and how does the construal of benefits change over time? *Prospective studies* (e.g., McCrae & Costa, 1993) allow the clear identification of what individuals were like before the occurrence of traumatic events. Studies of children and adolescents that include attention to the possibility of growth may yield a look at the times of innocence (i.e., before experience with, and perhaps knowledge of, traumatic events and the effects these events may have). Werner's (1989) work has addressed some of these issues, but by focusing on high-risk children, she has studied those who might have already been traumatized while very young. But the general longitudinal approach will offer useful answers to how the processes of growth from trauma unfold over time.

The relationship of *temperament and personality variables* to growth following exposure to trauma is an area that requires more answers. Our preliminary examination of the relationship between growth following trauma and personality variables suggests that individuals who are optimistic or extroverted are slightly more likely to perceive benefits arising from the crises with which they have had to cope (correlations of approximately .25).

The interactive nature of trauma and personality variables is also an area for additional work. Our suggestion is that the relationship between personality variables, such as self-efficacy, and the perception of growth arising from stressful situations is mutually influential. As one successfully struggles with great challenge, one's view of oneself becomes one of perceived competence, and the perceived increase in competence in turn is viewed as a benefit arising from coping with the challenge. It is not yet clear, however, which personality factors may be important and to what degree they are important in understanding the growth process.

A specific variable that has promise is *the degree of complexity* of an individual's belief systems (Morgan & Janoff-Bulman, 1992). People with more complex cognitive systems may be able to assimilate negative events more easily and be more able to perceive benefits from the struggle. Or, it may be that the individual's cognitive complexity may interact with the severity of the life circumstance in such a way that as cognitive complexity increases (with the increased ability to "absorb" the crisis), a higher degree of severity is required before the individual's cognitive systems are sufficiently threatened to force the changes that are required for growth to occur.

Related to the effect of cognitive complexity is the influence of the individual's *religious beliefs*. As we have suggested, religious beliefs, particularly the Judeo-Christian views that have predominated in the United States, are virtually immune to empirical disconfirmation.

Regardless of what happens at the empirical level, beliefs such as "God has a plan for everything; everything happens for a reason" and "I don't know why yet, but I was chosen to go through this for a reason" have a higher degree of immunity to disconfirmation by tragedy (Calhoun et al., 1992). The general empirical beliefs that may guide individuals about the world ("I think I can protect myself from harm, if I just take care") *can* be disproven by events (Janoff-Bulman, 1992). Available data indicate that spirituality and religion are areas in which survivors describe growth occurring in the struggle with trauma. Metaphysical concepts may also provide useful resources for coping with trauma (Koenig et al., 1988; Maton, 1989; McIntosh, 1991; Pargament, 1990; Wuthnow, 1992). The degree to which religious beliefs can help survivors assimilate traumatic events and grow from their difficulties seems a promising area for investigation.

SITUATIONAL VARIABLES

More needs to be known about *how contact with others affects the process of growth.* How much can others influence the process of growth, and if they can, by what processes do they do it?

The degree to which benefits may accrue vicariously, indirectly, to those who interact with the individual directly affected by the trauma (Miles et al., 1984) seems a fruitful area of inquiry. Bystanding observers, lay and professional caregivers, researchers, and others on the periphery of the tragedy may have the opportunity to grow vicariously. The suggestion of the indirect effect of trauma is not new (Janoff-Bulman & Timko, 1985, 1987), but it remains largely untested in the area of growth following trauma. One study reported that 85% of social workers providing support to victims of a railroad accident or oil-drilling accident found personal and professional benefits in their involvement (Hodgkinson & Shepherd, 1994). Vicarious trauma may produce some psychological growth, especially if it affects important schematic elements—those that represent the individual's central concerns (McCann & Pearlman, 1990)—and if the vicarious trauma is sufficiently salient to challenge some of the existing important cognitive elements. On the other hand, people who work with trauma victims are not necessarily any hardier or better copers, and there is some indication that the cumulative effect of working with trauma can be negative (Moran & Britton, 1994).

We began this book by identifying different areas in which individuals have reported growth, and we have spoken throughout the book about growth in the singular, but it is clear that *growth is not a single, unitary phenomenon*. Individuals facing one kind of difficulty may evidence growth in areas that differ from those experienced by individuals facing difficulty of a different kind (Taylor, Collins, Skokan, & Aspinwall, 1989). People with particular kinds of assumptive worlds may differ in the way they develop and construe benefits. The responses of the social support system, the prevailing zeitgeist, and the particular cultural context may encourage some kinds of growth and inhibit others, and particular personality styles may more likely be accompanied by some types of growth than by others.

Although beyond the scope of the model we proposed in Chapter 6, it will be useful to consider *the potential effect of higher-order ecological and cultural variables* on the degree to which individuals experience growth resulting from traumatic circumstances (Aldwin, 1994; Silver et al., 1983; Stroebe, Gergen, Gergen, & Stroebe, 1992). The cultural and historical milieu in which the trauma occurs may have effects, mediated by the immediate social network, on the degree to which growth from trauma may be facilitated or discouraged. Because such higher-order factors are less amenable to quantification and experimental analysis, it may not be possible for most investigators of the aftermath of trauma to readily evaluate their impact. Nevertheless, broad cultural factors should be noted as potential contributors to the specific instances in which one individual confronts and grows from trauma.

THE VALIDITY OF PERSONAL EXPERIENCE

Even if it is possible to clearly establish and describe the process, and perhaps the reasons or causes for them, *of what practical significance are the benefits perceived by survivors following an encounter with trauma?* From the viewpoint of the significant other, the professional caregiver, or even the individual affected, what difference does the construal of benefits make? There is some suggestion that the construal of benefits may, in some circumstances, be related to "objective" measures of psychological adjustment and well-being (Curbow et al., 1993; Goodhart, 1985; Smith, Houston, & Stucky, 1982), but this may not necessarily be the case (Carver et al., 1993; Joseph et al., 1993; Lehman et al., 1993). Is the growth that, for many people, follows the encounter with difficult life circumstances a good thing? Or, at the very least, is the perception of growth related to improved psychological functioning generally or to other indicators of satisfactory coping (Aldwin, 1994)?

Answers to these questions may depend on the degree of resolution that has occurred among people experiencing trauma, and how much they are still engaged in some process of coping with these events. Distress may coexist with perceptions of growth in people who are still coping with trauma, and it could be said that their perceptions of growth may be part of an ongoing process of positive reconstruing. After the passage of time, when distress is minimal, growth may be more closely related to good psychological functioning. Our model, presented in Chapter 6, suggests that different levels of growth occur over time and that longitudinal studies are needed to confirm this and the relationship of emotional distress, ongoing coping, growth, and psychological functioning.

The final unanswered question involves the possibility of cognitive bias in self-perceptions of growth. People seem to operate with a variety of cognitive biases that put a positive spin on judgments of objects, events, and people, and the ability to recall them accurately (Matlin & Stang, 1978). Positive biases also work to enhance one's self-perception (Brown, 1986; Klein & Kunda, 1993; Singer & Salovey, 1993; Swann, 1983; Taylor et al., 1993; Weinstein, 1980). Therefore, it would not be surprising to find such biases operating when a person's ability to manage, understand, and find meaning in events is severely tested by trauma. We should consider *whether the construal of benefits and the self-perception of growth simply represent another cognitive bias*, or is real.

We have described how survivors of trauma create life narratives that incorporate these events. Ross (1989) points out that this recon-structive process involves a tendency to remember events in such a way that there appears to be consistency in our actions then and what we are like now. Furthermore, this tendency is especially strong for positive characteristics of oneself. The process of growth, when it involves a clear distinction between an old self and a superior new self, appears to act contrary to this tendency to maintain consistency, although it could be a self-enhancement bias.

Results from a study recently completed (Calhoun, Tedeschi, Cann, Gill, & Burr, 1994) indicate that the tendency to report benefits arising from the struggle with difficult life events may be in part, but not exclusively, a function of a general cognitive bias to retroactively see one's life as always improving. Among college students reporting no significant traumatic events, self-reported positive life changes were generally in the small to moderate range, indicating a general tendency to see oneself as gradually getting better, more mature, or stronger. Among people reporting significant trauma, growth was reported to be greater. It appears that only under significantly negative circumstances will there be an impact on people's views of self, others, and life in general beyond a gradual personal growth that most people may perceive. It is also possible, however, that the greater perception of benefits by people in the trauma group may represent the consequences of a contrast effect. Individuals who have been exposed to a severe stressor may be rating greater perceived benefits because they are comparing their current state with a past state of great psychological distress, whereas individuals not reporting trauma do not have such a dramatically contrasting personal state with which to compare their current life.

Another way to determine whether growth perceived by people experiencing trauma is real is to compare their reports to the perceptions of "observers." One study (Park et al., in press) reveals a significant but low correlation ($r = .21$) between observers' and subjects' reports of growth as the result of traumatic events. This correlation rose somewhat ($r = .31$) when only "extremely close" observers' reports were compared to those experiencing the events. It should be noted, however, that some of the positive changes perceived by people experiencing trauma might not be easily ascertained, even by people intimately associated with someone experiencing these changes.

Another way to address the issue of the validity of reports of growth is to determine if individuals who have not experienced major trauma report the same kinds of positive change as those who have. Perceived growth could also be corroborated by external standards independent of anyone's perception, such as changes in abilities assessed independently. Finally, collecting prospective data might be the best way of measuring changes.

Which Perspective and Which Methods?

As much as any area of research within contemporary social and behavioral sciences, the matter of growth following trauma raises questions regarding the fundamental assumptions about *how to conduct research*. The prevailing viewpoint in the behavioral sciences, systematic empiricism, has been challenged, and the challengers have suggested that investigations of human beings and human actions cannot be done within the strict framework of traditional "science" (Bruner, 1990; Gergen, 1994; Lincoln & Guba, 1985). These challenges to the prevailing emphasis on objectivity and experimentation represent a viewpoint from which the actions of people are viewed as best investigated with a different "methodology," with a different set of assumptions.

These different views of how to approach the study of human actions are generally divisible into two categories (Bruner, 1986; Epstein, 1994). The first, which represents the perspective that most current researchers were taught and into which most were socialized, focuses on the use of logic, the empirical test of hypotheses, and the search for general causes (Bruner, 1986; Gergen, 1994). The other category is focused more on the experience of the individual, the reasons ascribed for behavior, and the ways in which individuals put together their own accounts of what happens to them (Bruner, 1986; Lincoln & Guba, 1985; Neimeyer, 1993). These two viewpoints have competing, even contradictory, assumptions about the nature of human beings and the utility of the traditional scientific method for the behavioral disciplines. However, it is preferable, at least at this point in the history of the behavioral disciplines in general, and of the study of growth following trauma in particular, to regard these two general modes of knowing as offering distinctive but useful ways of understanding the experience and behavior of individuals (Bruner, 1986).

This suggestion means that there will be a need for an increased tolerance of ambiguity, perhaps even of apparent contradictions, in the criteria used to evaluate the utility and "validity" of research efforts in the area of growth following trauma. It is desirable to encourage the employment of both quantitative methodologies, which are derived from the tradition of systematic empiricism that has prevailed in the social sciences (particularly psychology), and qualitative methodologies, which are not as compatible (if at all) with the prevailing assumptions of systematic empiricism.

The model we have proposed in Chapter 6 can serve as a starting point for the generation of qualitative investigations, and also offer a point of departure for quantitative studies of growth following trauma. Although it is beyond our scope to describe methodologies in detail, below we offer general suggestions for the study of growth.

QUALITATIVE APPROACHES

The use of extensive interviews with individuals who have direct experience, either of their own in the struggle with major stressors or in the role of observers of others who struggle, is an important step for further understanding. The transcription and subsequent analysis or coding of the interview data (Lincoln & Guba, 1985; Strauss, 1987), for example, represent a qualitative approach that is compatible with the training of many contemporary investigators. The evaluation of narratives and accounts that individuals make of their experience with trauma is also an avenue that is potentially fruitful, but that can represent a significant challenge for researchers who have not been trained within this particular framework. Nevertheless, potentially useful sources are available to serve as guides (e.g., Lincoln & Guba, 1985; Riessman, 1993; Sarbin, 1986; Strauss, 1987) for individuals who want to embark on this kind of research.

The use of these kinds of qualitative and narrative approaches, however, requires a willing suspension of belief in the singular authority of the traditional scientific method. At the very least, it requires an increased tolerance for studies that simply attempt to describe and summarize the experience of individuals without trying to test quantitative hypotheses designed to identify general "laws," which are independent of the individual's experience or of the context. Within the framework of qualitative studies and their guiding assumptions, the debate over the degree to which growth is illusory or real, and the degree to which such illusions contribute to mental health (Colvin & Block, 1994; Shedler, Mayman, & Manis, 1993; Taylor & Brown, 1994), becomes less meaningful. The individual's own understanding of what has happened in the struggle with major life challenges is regarded as a valid interpretation of what has happened, even if the interpretation may not necessarily provide direct information on how other individuals will understand their experiences. We suggest that the greater use of qualitative and narrative approaches can teach us much about the growth that many individuals experience following major crises.

QUANTITATIVE APPROACHES

At the same time, however, and perhaps in a way that represents a contradictory and paradoxical recommendation, we think it is useful to also proceed with investigations that take a traditional empirical, quantitative approach. Although the viewpoint of the individual experiencing the trauma is clearly valid, so is the viewpoint of the social or behavioral scientist whose interest is in evaluating the degree to which the experience and claim of growth is or is not accompanied systematically by changes in external standards of growth. Furthermore, systematic quantification may help us better understand the way in which the growth experienced by the individual may be related to antecedents and concomitants, and how growth and other factors may serve to reinforce one another and perhaps even "cause" growth.

Quantitative measures of perceptions of benefit or growth can be approached in at least two ways. Existing measures of psychological maturity or competence may be used to assess the status of people after coping with traumatic events to determine whether their behavior appears to have changed from previous functioning levels or differs from people of similar characteristics who have not experienced the trauma. Another way to quantitatively measure these changes is by asking questions about or requesting ratings of aspects of oneself affected by coping with trauma (Carver, Scheier, & Weintraub, 1989). Some measures have been developed recently that attempt to do this (Joseph et al., 1993; Park et al., in press; Tedeschi & Calhoun, in press).

One measure was developed by Joseph et al. (1993) for the purpose of determining changes experienced by survivors of a cruise ship disaster. The measure was designed to assess both positive and negative responses. The positive change items had good internal consistency (Cronbach's α = .83). Scores on these positive items were unrelated to measures of psychological symptoms and to social support, but modestly (r = .37) correlated with self-esteem.

Two measures that have been developed to assess positive life changes among people who have coped with any type of trauma are the Post Traumatic Growth Inventory (PTGI) (Tedeschi & Calhoun, in press) and the Stress-Related Growth Scale (SRGS) (Park et al., in press).

The Post Traumatic Growth Inventory

This scale (see Appendix) is composed of 21 items, including factors of New Possibilities, Relating to Others, Personal Strength, Appreciation of Life, and Spiritual Change. Internal consistency is $\alpha = .90$ and test-retest reliability over 8 weeks is $r = .71$. Females who experience trauma tend to report more perceived benefits than do males on all factors except New Possibilities. People experiencing positive events and those reporting negative events both reported perceiving benefits (Tedeschi, Calhoun, & Page, 1992). People experiencing severe trauma report greater change than do those who have not had extremely traumatic experiences. The PTGI is not related to social desirability and is modestly correlated with optimism and extroversion (Tedeschi & Calhoun, in press).

The Stress-Related Growth Scale

This scale is composed of 50 items that include positive changes in social relationships, personal resources, and coping skills. Internal consistency is $\alpha = .95$ and test-retest reliability over 2 weeks is $r = .81$. As with the PTGI, females tend to report more growth than males. More growth has been reported in response to positive rather than negative events with this scale, and people instructed to describe the growth they experienced over the previous year, rather than a specific event, reported the most growth of all. However, it is not known what sort of events were experienced during this time. The SRGS is not correlated with social desirability, and for negative events, reported growth was related to increases in optimism, positive affect, and satisfaction with social support over 6 months (Park et al., in press).

Although both of these measures hold promise, they need to be tested in a wide array of settings with a wide variety of people who are coping with a wide range of difficult life circumstances. So the question as to how to measure possible growth following a trauma can be answered by saying that there are useful possibilities available, but each may have significant limitations, at least for now. But the existence of these reliable measures will allow researchers in this area to assess growth over time, under different circumstances, and among different kinds of people.

A Research Strategy

To address the questions outlined in this chapter, researchers in this area need to do longitudinal and, ideally, prospective studies of different age groups confronting various traumatic events. Personality traits and coping strategies need to be assessed throughout this period. Outcome measures of growth, both qualitative and quantitative, need to be taken at various intervals from both the people themselves and from those who observe them. Other measures of adjustment, psychological functioning, altered constructs and schemas, and wisdom or maturity should be included. Because virtually all people confront some degree of trauma if a long-enough time span is considered, comparisons should be made between people for whom traumas significantly challenge established patterns of thinking and behaving and those who are not challenged in these ways. Using this strategy, the role of nonnormative events in personality development may be distinguished from more common or predictable life transitions.

GUIDEPOSTS FOR PEOPLE
CHALLENGED BY TRAUMA

I'm honestly not sure what would have happened to me if I hadn't come here [grief support group].

—Bereaved mother

The focus of this book has been on traumatic events, how personal growth can follow these events, how others may be helpful to someone who is encountering a major trauma, and on issues related to research and theory. In this chapter, we will speak directly to people who have experienced traumatic events. Here, more than in any other chapter, we draw primarily on our clinical work with individuals who have had to face major difficulties in life. We hope that professionals will use this chapter by providing it directly to clients or by using it to supplement information in other sections of the book. This chapter will be somewhat redundant with earlier chapters, but our intent here is to directly address people challenged by traumatic events.

Our goal is to help individuals challenged by traumatic events learn what they can do, not only to cope successfully with these events, but also to allow the struggle to have the transformative effects that we have been discussing in the preceding chapters. People reading this chapter who are at the beginning of their struggle and for whom the trauma is fresh may react with some incredulity to our suggestions.

This chapter may be less useful to them than to those for whom the dramatic occurrences connected to the trauma have receded into the past. Our aim is not to convince people early in the coping process that a transformative experience is possible or even expected for them. As we noted in Chapter 7, to introduce this notion to someone who is in "survival mode" is futile and may be counterproductive. Such people may wish to return to this material months or years from now when the initial coping has been accomplished and such an outcome seems possible.

Experience Is the Teacher

Challenged people need to recognize first that a transformative experience is not something that can be forced. Rather, people must put themselves in the position to learn not merely intellectually but experientially. "Knowing" the things that traumatized people learn takes place with a great deal of emotion. It is clear that one of the problems in treating people with posttraumatic stress disorder, for example, is that what has been learned from the horrible experience has taken root at a deep emotional level and thus is very resistant to change. Similarly, positive transformations are experienced at a deep emotional level, and this is in part what makes the changes so powerful for many individuals. Even Reinhold Niebuhr, who wrote the serenity prayer, had to learn the lessons of suffering more profoundly when he endured pain at the end of his life (Shinn, 1986). Challenged people cannot be helped simply by being told of the many ways in which trauma can lead to growth. The lessons that can lead to growth must be learned experientially. To provide guidance for challenged people, our suggestions fall into two broad categories: how to deal with reactions that tend to short-circuit this process and how to allow transformative lessons to be learned.

A Willingness to Accept and Endure

The first suggestion for the survivor of trauma is that growth is more likely if one can learn to accept and endure the immediate consequences of the challenging event. From our discussion of the process of growth in Chapter 6, we see that there are certain tasks that may be necessary for most people struggling with trauma. One is to be able to give up attempts at "primary control," that is, attempts to reverse the effects of the trauma, where such reversal is clearly impossible. Eventually, the affected individual must have a *willingness to accept* some aspects of the situation as unchangeable.

At the same time, however, this acceptance may have its most powerful effect on those very people who are most likely to attempt to make the changes that could result in a reversal of fortune. These people may have personal styles that lead them to have strong confidence in their abilities (e.g., a high level of self-efficacy), and they find themselves devoting a great deal of effort to the demands that the consequences of the events make on them. These efforts serve as a reminder that they still have considerable strength, and perhaps more strength than they realized. People must also be willing to *endure* a significant period of rumination. This rumination is experienced as searching and, for a long time, not finding ways to manage or understand the event. The need to endure and accept what is inevitable, of course, can represent growth that results from the struggle—here we are suggesting that to the extent that you, the challenged person, can summon up the capacity *not* "to just do something, but simply sit there," you will be increasing the possibility that positive changes can occur.

The Challenge Perspective

Setting new goals, even small ones, introduces people to possibilities for renewed action and success following an encounter with a traumatic set of circumstances. It also makes clear that the traumatic events can be treated as survivable challenges rather than tragic losses. Moving to *a perspective of the event as a challenge* appears to be a helpful step. Although responding to this challenge may demand a fighting spirit, anger and hostility may not necessarily be helpful emotions. Setting attainable small goals and meeting them may demand much self-discipline, and a persistence unknown before may need to be developed. Because individual circumstances vary greatly, it is impractical for us to provide a general set of guidelines as to how to select achievable goals. But it is important that the goals be appropriate to the context, realistically achievable, and ones toward which the challenged individual is willing to work. One of the people we have interviewed, for example, whose accident placed him permanently in a wheelchair, continued with the goal of being a champion weightlifter, a goal that required only the modification of which competitions he trained for and entered from then on.

Searching for Humor

Humor may also be helpful in this process because it can relieve emotional distress and even provide a measure of stress relief and temporary physical comfort. Not all people can generate humor successfully, and some individuals simply do not regard many things as funny. Most people, however, should "seek out the funny." Our recommendation is that you make searching out the funny things a systematic part of how you deal with the major loss. This recommendation seems so obvious as to be almost trite. However, our experience suggests that a *systematic* search and purposeful exposure to funny things is something that most people coping with major trauma do not do. When individuals are depressed and sad, they are less likely to appreciate the humor in things. Nevertheless, we are suggesting that you seek out the columnists, authors, television programs, movies, or any readily available humor and make it a part of your regular routine. In particular, to the extent that your individual sense of humor is accepting of it, search for humor that directly addresses you and your struggle in some way. Do not wait for humor to hit you—go looking for it and share it with others. As a boy with cancer told his physician, people's willingness to laugh with him showed him that there is hope (Komp, 1993).

Needing and Serving Others

Being told how to change is not enough. You will also need to rely on *information and advice from others.* In Chapter 7, we discussed the usefulness of support from others, and these connections may be crucial for the vast majority of people experiencing traumatic events. Accepting help from others is an experience in humility and intimacy that tends to produce some of the positive changes we have described in this book. The process of growing from trauma is both an intrapersonal and interpersonal experience, and both elements must be present and nurtured. The intrapersonal aspects occur during the process of acceptance and wrestling with the possible meaning of what has happened. The interpersonal aspects occur during times when help from others is accepted and when specific problem-solving approaches are learned from others. The interpersonal realm also plays a role during the time when your life narrative is reshaped. The "story" that you develop to describe and make sense out of tragedy may be a crucial component in seeing positive outcomes in the negative experience. This process can be furthered by telling and retelling to others the story of the trauma and the place it occupies in your life.

A powerful method of developing the story is through writing. For many people, writing about life traumas can be a great emotional release, help organize information, and encourage the process of remembering and healing. It is best to follow certain guidelines to derive the greatest benefit from the writing experience. First, write continuously without worrying about grammar, spelling, or sentence structure. Second, write about the deepest thoughts and feelings associated with the experience. Third, write about present feelings and thoughts as well as those that occurred at the time of the event. People who engage in this exercise often feel more depressed immediately after the writing, but over a few months, they experience more positive emotions and outlook as well as better physical health (Pennebaker, 1990).

The interpersonal realm becomes vitally important when it is discovered that one can be of assistance to others. However, for this discovery to occur, you need to *seek out opportunities to be of use to others, in particular those people who have more recently had to face similar circumstances.* As you take advantage of opportunities to be useful to others, you may well find that your altruism can provide meaning, purpose, and a clear demonstration of the strength you have that has persisted despite the stress and loss.

Being around others also prevents the development of isolation, loneliness, and the impression that "my circumstances are the worst." Self-pity is more easily avoided, and inspiration through others becomes possible. The recognition that one is among many people who have suffered misfortune will dispel the notion that fate has singled you out. At the same time, taking responsibility for managing the efforts involved is crucial. Help from others must be balanced by sometimes enormous personal efforts to manage the difficult situation. Being around others may also put you in social situations or in contact with people you never would have encountered otherwise, and this can open up the possibility for change.

Support groups for people who have faced difficulties similar to yours may be a context in which you can both be helped and provide help. Although support groups are not everyone's "cup of tea," our suggestion is that if this possibility is one you find potentially useful, you investigate what is available in your community. Sample what appeals to you and stay with groups you find useful. Remember, as you participate, that such groups represent opportunities for you to learn and receive, and also for you to teach and give.

An Active Search
for the Gains in the Losses

Another aspect of the process of transformation involves the changes in thought patterns referred to in our model in Chapter 6. People sometimes reflect on what has been lost because of the trauma and find it difficult to appreciate what remains. Although much of what happens in the wake of trauma involves loss, *you need to stay open to the possibility that some losses may represent positive change*. Sometimes people even find that what has been lost was a restriction in a way they had not previously realized. For example, Jerry, the man we quoted at the beginning of this book, found that his single-minded pursuit of a music career had left him with undiscovered talents in other areas and relationships that were not nurtured. His loss made it possible for him to develop other talents and to nurture the important relationships in his life. Trauma inevitably produces major losses, but search out those losses that, viewed from a different perspective, may represent an opportunity for positive change.

Being set back by a traumatic event can also change the way people view their relationships, their work, and the world around them.

Cultivating a more careful, deliberate perception of things can bring into focus aspects previously unnoticed, beauty unappreciated, and possibilities unrealized. These possibilities can be considered and chosen if one takes the risk and responsibility for this choice. Existential lessons are learned: Confronted with apparently *more limitations,* one can feel *more free* because the available choices are not artificially restricted by oneself.

Consideration of spiritual matters may be related to this existential learning, and a *spiritual self-assessment* is a useful exercise during times of adversity. This is not an exercise that will be either useful or meaningful to every person. For many, it is a natural consequence of an encounter with major tragedy or loss, but for others, attending consciously to spiritual or religious matters may prove a helpful foundation for some of the growth that may follow a major life crisis. The spiritual considerations, religious issues, and major existential questions are matters on which you may want to consciously focus, at least to determine if these are matters that seem relevant to you. If they are, then we suggest that you welcome the questions and wrestle with them.

One way in which these recommendations that we are making for the challenged person can be used is to make a listing of these various matters and determine how these ways of proceeding can be integrated into life. Rather than waiting for these particular issues to be raised spontaneously by circumstance, you can actively address them.

Readings in Transformation

In the remainder of this chapter, we provide a short list and brief description of some of the books written by or for people overcoming traumas. They are written from different perspectives and for a variety of readers, and they focus on the broader question of how to cope with trauma, but they can be guides for finding benefits and nurturing personal growth during the difficult journey through tragedy.

Although not focused primarily on the issues of growth and transformation, *Aftershock: Surviving the Delayed Effects of Trauma, Crisis, and Loss* (Slaby, 1989) contains many specific recommendations for navigating crises so that the person will be in a position to discover the growth that is possible. Slaby assumes that people can live after trauma "happier, more fulfilled, and wiser" (p. xv) if they take care of themselves properly during the period of "aftershock" that can affect them for a long time. He briefly describes reactions to war, crime, and various personal, social, and occupational events, and describes various modalities of psychotherapy, drug therapy, and self-help regimens.

Watersheds: Mastering Life's Unpredictable Crises (Lauer & Lauer, 1988) also provides insights on confronting life events with an eye toward personal benefit and growth. In this book, information is presented in the form of stories of people's experiences that illustrate the authors' points. These are finally summarized in 10 "life principles": taking responsibility for yourself; affirming your own worth; balancing self-concern with other-concern; finding and using resources; reframing; practicing silver-lining thinking; persevering; more carefully attending to the environment; periodically restructuring one's life; and developing the hardy personality (discussed in Chapter 4 of this volume).

A more intellectual account of resilience in the face of trauma, as well as rapidly changing social realities, is found in Robert Lifton's (1993) book, *The Protean Self: Human Resilience in an Age of Fragmentation*. For the person concerned with possibilities for transformation, the interviews with "proteans" (people who are capable of changing themselves as a response to crisis) are most interesting. Lifton focuses on social activists, civic leaders, poor African Americans, and Christian fundamentalists, but the common theme of personal trauma and transformation comes through in the discussions with people of all social positions, and all appear to be trying to find meaning and to create narratives that account for the remarkable transformations they have accomplished.

Focusing more specifically on one type of trauma is *The Resilient Self: How Survivors of Troubled Families Rise Above Adversity* (Wolin & Wolin, 1993). This book takes the viewpoint that family troubles can be fertile ground for growth, and this is reflected in the titles of the two sections that comprise the book: "Pain and Opportunity" and "Seven Resiliences." The authors take the work on resilient children (described in Chapter 4 of this volume) and extend it to a "challenge model" (vs. "damage model") of response to living in a troubled family. Although the book focuses on family problems as traumas, much of what is discussed has wider applicability. The authors describe how insights, independence, relationships, initiative, creativity, humor, and morality can be developed out of hurtful experiences.

Another book that focuses on one type of trauma, *Seven Choices: Taking the Steps to New Life After Losing Someone You Love* (Neeld, 1990), describes the grieving process in terms of active choices rather than something that just happens to people. As we mentioned earlier, the use of a more active coping strategy that allows a person to appreciate that he or she has choices in spite of tragedy is useful in setting the stage for growth.

A classic and harrowing account of this strategy is found in *Man's Search for Meaning: An Introduction to Logotherapy* (Frankl, 1963). Most of the book is an autobiographical account of Frankl's experiences in a Nazi concentration camp. One effect this book may have is to provide the perspective that one's own trauma may not be nearly as horrendous as Frankl's. But the most important thing that may be learned is the existential perspective that meaning can be found in suffering, and in this way even the worst suffering can be endured. This is no "cookbook" on how to grow through trauma, but it is full of wisdom.

A recent book based on interviews with Holocaust survivors who have adjusted particularly well is *Against All Odds* (Helmreich, 1992). Ten "general traits" of people able to lead positive and useful lives after the war parallel what we have described in preceding chapters: flexibility, assertiveness, tenacity, optimism, intelligence, distancing ability, group consciousness, assimilating the knowledge that one has survived, finding meaning in one's life, and courage. It is instructive to read how these personal characteristics and approaches to life have been put into action by these survivors.

A more recent autobiographical account of trauma is provided by the novelist, poet, and playwright Reynolds Price. In *A Whole New Life* (Price, 1994), he recounts the events of his bout with cancer. In the hands of an experienced and masterful writer, this personal narrative contains the elements of the unique and the universal, as discussed in Chapter 7. In his foreword, Price remarks that to him, his trauma seems like "total war," and although he does not claim any "special wisdom" from this experience, he hopes that others might benefit from his recounting, because "in my worst times I'd have given a lot to hear from veterans of the kind of ordeal I was trapped in" (p. vii). Perhaps what is most useful about the book as a whole is the demonstration of what creative expression, mostly writing, can offer to people struggling with trauma. Through his calendars and retrospective on the events of 10 years, Price develops the story that can encompass the terrifying and painful events and comes to a conclusion reflected in the title. To live through a trauma, a person has to grieve for the old self that has been lost, then move on "to be somebody else, the next viable you—a stripped-down whole other clear-eyed person, realistic as a sawed-off shotgun and thankful for air, not to speak of the human kindness you'll meet if you get normal luck" (p. 183). What Price offers is valuable to any caregiver as well because he gives many examples of both kindness and thoughtlessness that he received at the hands of friends and professionals.

A widely read book, *Necessary Losses* (Viorst, 1986), reviews many life difficulties and how they can be springboards to growth. There is a mixture here of developmental transitions similar to those described by Erikson (1950) and traumas, especially bereavement. This is not a "how-to" book but a readable exposition of what most of us have confronted and can expect to confront in life, and how to find meaning in personal development. In some ways, the book is a description of how people develop the wisdom of the aged.

Three books that deal specifically with spiritual and religious themes are the classic *A Grief Observed* (Lewis, 1963), the very popular *When Bad Things Happen to Good People* (Kushner, 1981), and the "new age" *Fire in the Soul: A New Psychology of Spiritual Optimism* (Borysenko, 1993). C. S. Lewis's book is a journal of his thoughts after the death of his wife. The reader journeys with him as his religious faith is questioned and eventually renewed. Kushner also asks the questions that haunt many people after the experience of traumatic events, most of which can be reduced to "Why?" He reaches the conclusion that many tragedies happen randomly, and that there is an important role that religion has to play in giving strength and moral force so that people choose to overcome terrible events and help others. Borysenko also addresses the question of why bad things happen, and draws the conclusion that suffering allows people "to see God with new eyes" (p. 32). She then leads the reader on an exploration of spiritual themes about suffering found in a variety of religions, and in literature and psychology.

Finally, a new resource for people who have suffered traumatization and are seeking to recover is the organization called "Gift From Within." This nonprofit group was formed in 1993 in Camden, Maine. It develops educational materials, including videotapes and books, and maintains a listing of people who wish to participate in a national network of mutual support.

Conclusions

Several common themes emerge from these accounts of trauma, its benefits, and the process of moving from the former to the latter. Even the worst traumas can result in transformation. The process is a long one, perhaps with no end. Supportive others are very helpful in this journey, but eventually, one's own peace must be made with the event. This peace involves giving up many things: old assumptions; hopes; belief systems; and, in particular, notions of invulnerability and personal power, and harsh judgments of self and others. Paradoxically, a new sense of power must be nurtured: the determination to extract the good from living and to actively contribute to it. Confronting spiritual issues is almost always an aspect of this process of transformation, and comfort is often found in decisions to accept and serve.

It is important to recognize that for some people, extreme trauma may require years of transformation after the initial process of successful coping has been completed. Subsequent life events can reactivate the old feelings of distress associated with the traumatic event (Wilson, 1989), but this does not mean that the process is starting over, or that a setback has occurred. Treatment for trauma may never be complete (Herman, 1992), and it is important to remember the ways of thinking and acting that have been relied on to foster recovery so that they can be returned to when necessary.

APPENDIX

THE POST TRAUMATIC GROWTH INVENTORY

Indicate for each of the statements below the degree to which this change occurred in your life as a result of your crisis, using the following scale.

1 = I did not experience this change as a result of my crisis.
2 = I experienced this change to a *very small degree* as a result of my crisis.
3 = I experienced this change to a *small degree* as a result of my crisis.
4 = I experienced this change to a *moderate degree* as a result of my crisis.
5 = I experienced this change to a *great degree* as a result of my crisis.
6 = I experienced this change to a *very great degree* as a result of my crisis.

1. My priorities about what is important in life. (IV)
2. I'm more likely to try to change things which need changing. (I)
3. An appreciation for the value of my own life. (IV)
4. A feeling of self-reliance. (III)
5. A better understanding of spiritual matters. (V)
6. Knowing that I can count on people in times of trouble. (II)
7. A sense of closeness with others. (II)
8. Knowing I can handle difficulties. (III)
9. A willingness to express my emotions. (II)
10. Being able to accept the way things work out. (III)
11. Appreciating each day. (IV)
12. Having compassion for others. (II)
13. I'm able to do better things with my life. (I)
14. New opportunities are available which wouldn't have been otherwise. (I)
15. Putting effort into my relationships. (II)
16. I have a stronger religious faith. (V)
17. I discovered that I'm stronger than I thought I was. (III)
18. I learned a great deal about how wonderful people are. (II)
19. I developed new interests. (I)
20. I accept needing others. (II)

21. I established a new path for my life.   (I)

NOTE: Scale is scored by adding all responses. Factors are scored by adding responses to items on factors.

Factor I: New Possibilities
Factor II: Relating to Others
Factor III: Personal Strength
Factor IV: Appreciation of Life
Factor V: Spiritual Change

The Development of the
Post Traumatic Growth Inventory (PTGI)

ITEM DEVELOPMENT

The first step in developing the PTGI was a general review of studies of perceived benefits. Thirty-four items were generated.

Factor Analysis

A factor analysis was performed on these items using a principal component extraction and varimax rotation, yielding six factors. These accounted for 55% of the common variance and included 21 items that loaded greater than .5 on one of the five factors without loading .4 or greater on any other factor. There was a Pearson product-moment correlation of $r = .98$ between total score based on the 21-item version of the PTGI and the total score based on 34 items.

Norms

Females reported more benefits ($M = 75.18$, $SD = 21.24$) than males ($M = 67.77$, $SD = 22.07$), $t(1, 590) = 3.94$, $p < .001$. Females also scored higher than males on every factor except New Possibilities.

Internal Consistency and Test-Retest Reliability

The internal consistency of the PTGI is $\alpha = .90$, and for the factors, α ranged from .67 to .85. Corrected item-scale correlations ($r = .35$ to $r = .63$) indicated that all items are measuring a similar underlying construct, but none is overly redundant with the others. The Pearson product-moment correlations among the subscales ranged from $r = .27$ to $r = .52$.

In a sample of 28 persons, the test-retest reliability over a 2-month period for the 21 items was $r = .71$.

CONSTRUCT VALIDITY

Some discriminant validity work has been done with samples ranging from $N = 318$ to $N = 449$. Only the Appreciation of Life factor is related to social desirability, but the modest relationship ($r = -.15$) indicates that persons reporting more appreciation of life are less likely to present themselves in a socially desirable fashion. The PTGI is modestly correlated with optimism ($r = .23$), as measured by the Life Orientation Test (Scheier & Carver, 1985). Among the "Big Five" factors of personality, as measured by the NEO Personality Inventory (Costa & McCrae, 1985), the PTGI is most strongly related to Extroversion ($r = .29$). It is also related at more modest levels to Openness to Experience ($r = .21$), Agreeableness ($r = .18$), and Conscientiousness ($r = .16$). There is no relationship with Neuroticism, indicating that persons who report benefits from experiencing trauma are neither more nor less well adjusted than persons who do not report these benefits.

Persons experiencing severe trauma reported more benefits than those who did not, on the PTGI score and on the following factors: New Possibilities, Relating to Others, Personal Strength, and Appreciation of Life. Females who experienced trauma received higher scores on the PTGI ($M = 90.26$) than did males ($M = 73.48$). Complete data on scale development and validity studies are reported in Tedeschi and Calhoun (in press).

REFERENCES

Abbott, D. A., & Meredith, W. H. (1986). Strengths of parents with retarded children. *Family Relations, 35,* 371-375.

Abrahamson, L. Y., Metalsky, G. I., & Alloy, L. B. (1989). Hopelessness depression: A theory-based subtype of depression. *Psychological Review, 96,* 358-372.

Abrams, F. R. (1989). Medical-ethical perspectives on human suffering. In R. Taylor & J. Watson (Eds.), *They shall not hurt* (pp. 89-105). Boulder: Colorado Associated University Press.

Adams, P. R., & Adams, G. R. (1984). Mount Saint Helens ashfall. *American Psychologist, 39,* 252-260.

Adler, A. (1943). Neuropsychiatric complications in victims of Boston's Coconut Grove disaster. *Journal of the American Medical Association, 123,* 1098-1101.

Affleck, G., Allen, D. A., Tennen, H., McGrade, B. J., & Ratzan, S. (1985). Causal and control cognitions in parents' coping with chronically ill children. *Journal of Social and Clinical Psychology, 3,* 367-377.

Affleck, G., Tennen, H., & Gershman, K. (1985). Cognitive adaptations to high-risk infants: The search for mastery, meaning, and protection from future harm. *American Journal of Mental Deficiency, 89,* 653-656.

Aldwin, C. M. (1994). *Stress, coping, and development.* New York: Guilford.

Aldwin, C. M., Levenson, M. R., & Spiro, A. (1994). Vulnerability and resilience to combat exposure: Can stress have life-long effects? *Psychology and Aging, 9,* 34-44.

Alexander, V. (1991). *Words I never thought to speak: Stories of life in the wake of suicide.* New York: Lexington Books.

American Psychiatric Association. (1994). *Diagnostic and statistical manual of mental disorders* (4th ed.). Washington, DC: Author.

Anderson, C. A. (1989). The severely physically disabled: A subjective account of suffering. In R. Taylor & J. Watson (Eds.), *They shall not hurt* (pp. 107-124). Boulder: Colorado Associated University Press.

Anderson, J. R. (1985). *Cognitive psychology and its implications* (2nd ed.). New York: Freeman.

Andreasen, N. L., & Norris, A. S. (1972). Long-term adjustment and adaptation mechanisms in severely burned adults. *Journal of Nervous and Mental Disease, 154,* 352-362.

Andrykowski, M. A. (1992, August). *Positive psychosocial adjustment among cancer survivors.* Paper presented at the annual meeting of the American Psychological Association, Washington, DC.

Antonovsky, A. (1987). *Unraveling the mystery of health: How people manage stress and stay well.* San Francisco: Jossey-Bass.

Antonucci, T. C., & Jackson, J. S. (1990). The role of reciprocity in social support. In B. R. Sarason, I. G. Sarason, & G. R. Pierce (Eds.), *Social support: An interactional view* (pp. 173-198). New York: John Wiley.

Aristotle. (1970). *Poetics* (G. F. Else, Trans.). Ann Arbor: University of Michigan Press.

Auerhahn, N. C., Laub, D., & Peskin, H. (1993). Psychotherapy with Holocaust survivors. *Psychotherapy, 30,* 434-442.

Averill, J. R., & Nunley, E. P. (1992). *Voyages of the heart: Living an emotionally creative life.* New York: Free Press.

Balk, D. E., & Hogan, N. S. (in press). Religion, spirituality, and bereaved adolescents. In D. W. Adams & E. J. Deveau (Eds.), *Helping children and adolescents: The impact of threat to their lives, dying, death, and bereavement.* Amityville, NY: Baywood.

Baltes, P. B., & Smith, J. (1990). Toward a psychology of wisdom and its ontogenesis. In R. J. Sternberg (Ed.), *Wisdom: Its nature, origins, and development* (pp. 87-120). Cambridge, UK: Cambridge University Press.

Bandura, A. (1977). Self-efficacy: Toward a unifying theory of behavioral change. *Psychological Review, 84,* 191-215.

Bandura, A. (1978). The self-system in reciprocal determinism. *American Psychologist, 33,* 344-358.

Bandura, A. (1982a). Self-efficacy mechanism in human agency. *American Psychologist, 37,* 122-147.

Bandura, A. (1982b). The psychology of chance encounters and life paths. *American Psychologist, 37,* 747-755.

Bandura, A. (1986). *Social foundations of thought and action: A social cognitive theory.* Englewood Cliffs, NJ: Prentice Hall.

Bandura, A. (1988). Self-efficacy conception of anxiety. *Anxiety Research, 1,* 77-98.

Bandura, A., Cioffi, D., Taylor, C. B., & Brouillard, M. E. (1988). Perceived self-efficacy in coping with cognitive stressors and opioid activation. *Journal of Personality and Social Psychology, 55,* 479-488.

Bandura, A., O'Leary, A., Taylor, C. B., Gauthier, J., & Gossard, D. (1987). Perceived self-efficacy and pain control: Opioid and nonopioid mechanisms. *Journal of Personality and Social Psychology, 53,* 563-571.

Barrera, M., Jr. (1988). Models of social support: Beyond the buffering hypothesis. In L. H. Cohen (Ed.), *Life events and psychological functioning* (pp. 211-236). Newbury Park, CA: Sage.

Baruch, R., & Stutman, S. (1992, August). Resilience: Searching for an interventive strategy. In H. Tomes (Chair), *The process of fostering resilience: Roles for psychologists and media.* Symposium conducted at the annual meeting of the American Psychological Association, Washington, DC.

Baumeister, R. F. (1991). *Meanings of life.* New York: Guilford.

Beardslee, W. R., & Podorefsky, D. (1988). Resilient adolescents whose parents have serious affective and other psychiatric disorders: Importance of self-understanding and relationships. *American Journal of Psychiatry, 145,* 63-69.

Berger, P. L. (1967). *The sacred canopy: Elements of a sociological theory of religion.* Garden City, NY: Doubleday.

Berger, R. (1988). Learning to survive and cope with human loss. *Social Work Today, 19*(34), 14-17.

Bergin, A. E. (1991). Values and religious issues in psychotherapy and mental health. *American Psychologist, 46,* 394-403.

Berlin, N. (1981). *The secret cause: A discussion of tragedy.* Amherst: University of Massachusetts Press.

Bijur, P. E., Wallston, K. A., Smith, C. A., Lifrak, S., & Friedman, S. A. (1993, August). *Gender differences in turning to religion for coping.* Paper presented at the annual meeting of the American Psychological Association, Washington, DC.

Birren, J. E., & Fisher, L. M. (1990). The elements of wisdom: Overview and integration. In R. J. Sternberg (Ed.), *Wisdom: Its nature, origins, and development* (pp. 317-332). Cambridge, UK: Cambridge University Press.

Borysenko, J. (1993). *Fire in the soul: A new psychology of spiritual optimism.* New York: Warner.

Bowker, J. (1970). *Problems of suffering in religions of the world.* New York: Cambridge University Press.

Bowlby, J. (1980). *Loss: Sadness and depression.* New York: Basic Books.

Brewin, C. R. (1984). Attributions for industrial accidents: Their relationship to rehabilitation outcome. *Journal of Social and Clinical Psychology, 2,* 156-164.

Brickman, P., Rabinowitz, V., Karuza, J., Coates, D., Cohn, E., & Kidder, L. (1982). Models of helping and coping. *American Psychologist, 37,* 368-384.

Brown, J. D. (1986). Evaluations of self and others: Self-enhancement biases in social judgments. *Social Cognition, 4,* 353-376.

Brueggemann, W. (1984). *The message of the Psalms.* Minneapolis, MN: Augsburg.

Bruner, J. (1986). *Actual minds, possible worlds.* Cambridge, MA: Harvard University Press.

Bruner, J. (1990). *Acts of meaning.* Cambridge, MA: Harvard University Press.

Burger, J. M. (1989). Negative reactions to increases in perceived personal control. *Journal of Personality and Social Psychology, 56,* 246-256.

Burt, M. R., & Katz, B. L. (1987). Dimensions of recovery from rape: Focus on growth outcomes. *Journal of Interpersonal Violence, 2,* 57-81.

Calhoun, K. S., & Atkeson, B. M. (1991). *Treatment of rape victims.* New York: Pergamon.

Calhoun, L. G., & Allen, B. G. (1991). Social reactions to the survivor of suicide in the family: A review of the literature. *Omega, 23,* 95-107.

Calhoun, L. G., & Tedeschi, R. G. (1989-1990). Positive aspects of critical life problems: Recollections of grief. *Omega, 20,* 265-272.

Calhoun, L. G., Tedeschi, R. G., Cann, A., Gill, M. J., & Burr, H. (1994). *Perceiving benefits: Negative events, positive events, and positive bias.* Manuscript submitted for publication.

Calhoun, L. G., Tedeschi, R. G., & Lincourt, A. (1992, August). *Life crises and religious beliefs: Changed beliefs or assimilated events?* Paper presented at the annual meeting of the American Psychological Association, Washington, DC.

Campbell, A. (1981). *The sense of well-being in America*. New York: McGraw-Hill.

Caplan, G. (1964). *Principles of preventive psychiatry*. New York: Basic Books.

Carver, C. S., Pozo, C., Harris, S. D., Noreiga, V., Scheier, M. F., Robinson, D. S., Ketcham, A. S., Moffat, F. L., & Clark, K. C. (1993). How coping mediates the effect of optimism on distress: A study of women with early stage breast cancer. *Journal of Personality and Social Psychology, 65*, 375-390.

Carver, C. S., & Scheier, M. F. (1981). *Attention and self-regulation*. New York: Springer-Verlag.

Carver, C. S., & Scheier, M. F. (1987, August). *Dispositional optimism, coping and stress*. Paper presented at the annual meeting of the American Psychological Association, New York.

Carver, C. S., Scheier, M. F., & Weintraub, J. K. (1989). Assessing coping strategies: A theoretically based approach. *Journal of Personality and Social Psychology, 56*, 267-283.

Church, J. S. (1974). The Buffalo Creek disaster: Extent and range of emotional and/or behavioral problems. *Omega, 5*, 61-63.

Collins, R. L., Taylor, S. E., & Skokan, L. A. (1990). A better world or a shattered vision? Changes in life perspectives following victimization. *Social Cognition, 8*, 263-285.

Colvin, C. R., & Block, J. (1994). Do positive illusions foster mental health? An examination of the Taylor and Brown formulation. *Psychological Bulletin, 116*, 3-20.

Constantine, L. (1986). *Family paradigms*. New York: Guilford.

Costa, P. T., Jr., & McCrae, R. R. (1985). *NEO Personality Inventory manual*. Odessa, FL: Psychological Assessment Resources.

Costa, P. T., Jr., & McCrae, R. R. (1986). Personality stability and its implications for clinical psychology. *Clinical Psychology Review, 6*, 407-424.

Costa, P. T., Jr., & Widiger, T. A. (1994). *Personality disorders and the five-factor model of personality*. Washington, DC: American Psychological Association.

Coyne, J. C., & Downey, G. (1991). Social factors and psychopathology: Stress, social support, and coping processes. In *Annual review of psychology* (Vol. 42, pp. 401-425). Palo Alto, CA: Annual Reviews, Inc.

Coyne, J. C., Ellard, J. H., & Smith, D. A. F. (1990). Social support, interdependence, and the dilemmas of helping. In B. R. Sarason, I. G. Sarason, & G. R. Pierce (Eds.), *Social support: An interactional view* (pp. 129-149). New York: John Wiley.

Coyne, J. C., & Smith, D. A. F. (1994). Couples coping with a myocardial infarction: Contextual perspective on patient self-efficacy. *Journal of Family Psychology, 8*, 43-54.

Coyne, J. C., Wortman, C. B., & Lehman, D. R. (1988). The other side of support: Emotional overinvolvement and miscarried helping. In B. H. Gottlieb (Ed.), *Marshaling social support* (pp. 305-330). Newbury Park, CA: Sage.

Crowne, D. P., & Liverant, S. (1963). Conformity under varying conditions of personal commitment. *Journal of Abnormal and Social Psychology, 66*, 547-555.

Curbow, B., Somerfield, R., Baker, F., Wingard, J. R., & Legro, M. W. (1993). Personal changes, dispositional optimism, and psychological adjustment to bone marrow transplantation. *Journal of Behavioral Medicine, 16*, 423-443.

Cutrona, C. E. (1990). Stress and social support—In search of optimal matching. *Journal of Social and Clinical Psychology, 9*, 3-14.

Dakof, G. A., & Taylor, S. E. (1990). Victims' perceptions of social support: What is helpful from whom? *Journal of Personality and Social Psychology, 58*, 80-89.

Darvill, T. J., & Johnson, R. C. (1991). Optimism and perceived control of life events as related to personality. *Personality and Individual Differences, 12,* 951-954.

Davidson, L. M., Fleming, I., & Baum, A. (1986). Post-traumatic stress as a function of chronic stress and toxic experience. In C. R. Figley (Ed.), *Trauma and its wake: Traumatic stress theory research and intervention* (Vol. 2, pp. 57-77). New York: Brunner/Mazel.

Davis, R. G., & Friedman, L. N. (1985). The emotional aftermath of crimes and violence. In C. R. Figley (Ed.), *Trauma and its wake: The study and treatment of post-traumatic stress disorder* (Vol. 1, pp. 90-112). New York: Brunner/Mazel.

Diener, E. (1984). Subjective well-being. *Psychological Bulletin, 95,* 542-575.

Dienstbier, R. A. (1992). Mutual impacts of toughening on crises and losses. In L. Montada, S. Filipp, & M. J. Lerner (Eds.), *Life crises and experiences of loss in adulthood* (pp. 367-384). Hillsdale, NJ: Lawrence Erlbaum.

Dorman, L. (1994, May 17). To Azinger, cancer becomes a blessing. *New York Times.*

Downey, G., Silver, R. C., & Wortman, C. B. (1990). Reconsidering the attribution-adjustment relation following a major negative event: Coping with the loss of a child. *Journal of Personality and Social Psychology, 59,* 925-940.

Drabek, T. E., & Key, W. H. (1976). The impact of disaster on primary group linkages. *Mass Emergencies, 1,* 89-105.

Druss, R. G., & Douglas, C. J. (1988). Adaptive responses to illness and disability: Healthy denial. *General Hospital Psychiatry, 10,* 163-168.

Elder, G. H., Jr. (1979). Historical change in life patterns and personality. In P. B. Baltes & O. G. Brim (Eds.), *Life span development and behavior* (Vol. 2, pp. 117-159). New York: Academic Press.

Elder, G. H., Jr., & Clipp, E. C. (1989). Combat experience and emotional health: Impairment and resilience in later life. *Journal of Personality, 57,* 311-341.

Ell, K., & Dunkel-Schetter, C. (1994). Social support and adjustment to myocardial infarction, angioplasty, and coronary artery bypass surgery. In S. A. Shumaker & S. M. Czajkowski (Eds.), *Social support and cardiovascular disease* (pp. 301-332). New York: Plenum.

Epstein, S. (1973). The self-concept revisited, or a theory of a theory. *American Psychologist, 28,* 404-416.

Epstein, S. (1980). The self-concept: A review and the proposal of an integrated theory of personality. In E. Staub (Ed.), *Personality: Basic issues and current research* (pp. 81-132). Englewood Cliffs, NJ: Prentice Hall.

Epstein, S. (1990). The self-concept, the traumatic neurosis, and the structure of personality. In D. Ozer, J. M. Healy, Jr., & A. J. Stewart (Eds.), *Perspectives on personality* (Vol. 3, pp. 63-98). Greenwich, CT: JAI.

Epstein, S. (1994). Integration of the cognitive and the psychodynamic unconscious. *American Psychologist, 49,* 709-724.

Erikson, E. H. (1950). *Childhood and society.* New York: Norton.

Everstine, D. S., & Everstine, L. (1993). *The trauma response: Treatment for emotional injury.* New York: Norton.

Fisher, S., & Fisher, R. L. (1993). *The psychology of adaptation to absurdity.* Hillsdale, NJ: Lawrence Erlbaum.

Fiske, S. T., & Taylor, S. E. (1984). *Social cognition.* Reading, MA: Addison-Wesley.

Foa, E. B., Rothbaum, B. O., Riggs, D. S., & Murdock, T. B. (1991). Treatment of posttraumatic stress disorder in rape victims: A comparison between cognitive-behavioral procedures and counseling. *Journal of Consulting and Clinical Psychology, 59,* 715-723.

Folkman, S. (1984). Personal control and stress in the coping process: A theoretical analysis. *Journal of Personality and Social Psychology, 46,* 839-852.

Frankl, V. (1961). Logotherapy and the challenge of suffering. *Review of Existential Psychology and Psychiatry, 1,* 3-7.

Frankl, V. E. (1963). *Man's search for meaning: An introduction to logotherapy.* New York: Pocket Books.

Franklin, K. M., Janoff-Bulman, R., & Roberts, J. E. (1990). Long-term impact of parental divorce on optimism and trust: Changes in general assumptions or narrow beliefs? *Journal of Personality and Social Psychology, 59,* 743-755.

Fritz, G. K., Williams, J. R., & Amylon, M. (1988). After treatment ends: Psychosocial sequelae in pediatric cancer survivors. *American Journal of Orthopsychiatry, 58,* 552-561.

Fromm, E. (1947). *Man for himself.* New York: Holt, Rinehart & Winston.

Ganzini, L., McFarland, B. H., & Cutler, D. (1990). Prevalence of mental disorders after catastrophic financial loss. *Journal of Nervous and Mental Disease, 17,* 680-685.

Garbarino, J., Kostelny, K., & Durow, N. (1991). What children can tell us about living in danger. *American Psychologist, 46,* 376-383.

Garmezy, N. (1985). Stress resistant children: The search for protective factors. In J. E. Stevenson (Ed.), *Recent research in developmental psychopathology. Journal of Child Psychology and Psychiatry* (Book Suppl. No. 4). Oxford, UK: Pergamon.

Gergen, K. (1994). *Toward transformation in social knowledge* (2nd ed.). London: Sage.

Gibbons, F. X. (1986). Social comparison and depression: Company's effect on misery. *Journal of Personality and Social Psychology, 51,* 140-148.

Goodhart, D. E. (1985). Some psychological effects associated with positive and negative thinking about stressful event outcomes: Was Pollyanna right? *Journal of Personality and Social Psychology, 48,* 216-232.

Gore, P. M., & Rotter, J. B. (1963). A personality correlate of social action. *Journal of Personality, 31,* 58-64.

Gorkin, L., Follick, M. J., Wilkin, D. L., & Niaura, R. (1994). Social support and the progression and treatment of cardiovascular disease. In S. A. Shumaker & S. M. Czajkowski (Eds.), *Social support and cardiovascular disease* (pp. 281-299). New York: Plenum.

Gottlieb, B. H., & Wagner, F. (1991). Stress and support processes in close relationships. In J. Eckenrode (Ed.), *The social context of coping* (pp. 165-188). New York: Plenum.

Graham, B. (1981). *Till Armageddon: A perspective on suffering.* Minneapolis, MN: Grason.

Green, D. (1986, Summer). The origins of resilience. *Changes,* pp. 276-278.

Greenwald, A. G. (1980). The totalitarian ego: Fabrication and revision of personal history. *American Psychologist, 35,* 603-618.

Greven, P. (1990). *Spare the child.* New York: Knopf.

Hager, D. (1992). Chaos and growth. *Psychotherapy, 29,* 378-384.

Hall, C. M. (1986). Crisis as opportunity for spiritual growth. *Journal of Religion and Health, 25,* 8-17.

Hamera, E. K., & Shontz, F. C. (1978). Perceived positive and negative effects of life-threatening illness. *Journal of Psychosomatic Medicine, 22,* 419-424.

Hamilton, J. C., Greenberg, J., Pyszczynski, T., & Cather, C. (1993). A self-regulatory perspective on psychopathology and psychotherapy. *Journal of Psychotherapy Integration, 3,* 205-248.

Hannah, T. E. (1988, Summer). Hardiness and health behavior: The role of health concern as a moderator variable. *Behavioral Medicine*, pp. 59-63.

Harvey, J. H., Orbuch, T. L., Chwalisz, K. D., & Garwood, G. (1991). Coping with sexual assault: The roles of account-making and confiding. *Journal of Traumatic Stress, 4,* 515-531.

Harvey, J., Weber, A., & Orbuch, T. L. (1990). *Interpersonal accounts.* Cambridge, MA: Basil Blackwell.

Hastie, R. (1981). Schematic principles in human memory. In E. T. Higgins, C. P. Herman, & M. Zanna (Eds.), *Social cognition: The Ontario symposium* (Vol. 1, pp. 39-88). Hillsdale, NJ: Lawrence Erlbaum.

Healy, J. M., Jr. (1989). Emotional adaptation to life transitions: Early impact on integrative cognitive processes. In D. M. Buss & N. Cantor (Eds.), *Personality psychology: Recent trends and emerging directions* (pp. 115-127). New York: Springer-Verlag.

Helgeson, V. S. (1991). The effects of masculinity and social support on recovery from myocardial infarction. *Psychosomatic Medicine, 53,* 621-633.

Helgeson, V. S., & Taylor, S. E. (1993). Social comparisons and adjustment among cardiac patients. *Journal of Applied Social Psychology, 15,* 1171-1195.

Helmreich, W. B. (1992). *Against all odds: Holocaust survivors and the successful lives they made in America.* New York: Simon & Schuster.

Herbert, T. C., & Cohen, S. (1993). Stress and immunity in humans: A meta-analytic review. *Psychosomatic Medicine, 55,* 364-379.

Herman, J. L. (1992). *Trauma and recovery.* New York: Basic Books.

Hobfoll, S. E., Spielberger, C. D., Breznitz, S., Figley, C., Folkman, S., Lepper-Green, B., Meichenbaum, D., Milgram, N., Sandler, I., Sarason, I., & van der Kolk, B. (1991). War-related stress: Addressing the stress of war and other traumatic events. *American Psychologist, 46,* 848-855.

Hobfoll, S. E., & Vaux, A. (1993). Social support: Social resources and social context. In L. Goldberger & S. Breznitz (Eds.), *Handbook of stress: Theoretical and clinical aspects* (2nd ed., pp. 685-705). New York: Free Press.

Hodgkinson, P. E., & Shepherd, M. A. (1994). The impact of disaster support work. *Journal of Traumatic Stress, 7,* 587-600.

Hodgkinson, P. E., & Stewart, M. (1991). *Coping with catastrophe.* London: Routledge.

Holahan, C. J., & Moos, R. H. (1990). Life stressors, resistance factors, and improved psychological functioning: An extension of the stress resistance paradigm. *Journal of Personality and Social Psychology, 58,* 909-917.

Horowitz, M. J. (1975). Intrusive and repetitive thoughts after experimental stress: A summary. *Archives of General Psychiatry, 32,* 1457-1463.

Horowitz, M. J. (1976). *Stress response syndromes.* New York: Jason Aronson.

Horowitz, M. J. (1986). *Stress response syndromes* (2nd ed.). Northvale, NJ: Jason Aronson.

Houston, B. K., Bloom, L. J., Burish, T. G., & Cummings, E. M. (1978). Positive evaluation of stressful experiences. *Journal of Personality, 46,* 205-214.

Howard, G. S. (1989). *A tale of two stories: Excursions into a narrative approach to psychology.* Notre Dame, IN: Academic Publications.

Hoyt, T., Jr. (1978). What can Christianity do for me? In H. J. Young (Ed.), *Preaching on suffering and a God of love* (pp. 73-77). Philadelphia: Fortress Press.

Hurley, D. (1987, August). A sound mind in an unsound body. *Psychology Today,* pp. 34-43.

Janoff-Bulman, R. (1979). Characterological versus behavioral self-blame: Inquiries into depression and rape. *Journal of Personality and Social Psychology, 37,* 1798-1809.

Janoff-Bulman, R. (1989a). Assumptive worlds and the stress of traumatic events: Applications of the schema construct. *Social Cognition, 7,* 113-136.

Janoff-Bulman, R. (1989b). The benefits of illusions, the threat of disillusionment, and the limitations of inaccuracy. *Journal of Social and Clinical Psychology, 8,* 158-175.

Janoff-Bulman, R. (1992). *Shattered assumptions.* New York: Free Press.

Janoff-Bulman, R., & Timko, C. (1985). Working with victims: Changes in the researcher's assumptive world. In A. Baum & J. Singer (Eds.), *Advances in environmental psychology: Methods and environmental psychology* (Vol. 5, pp. 75-97). Hillsdale, NJ: Lawrence Erlbaum.

Janoff-Bulman, R., & Timko, C. (1987). Coping with traumatic life events. In C. R. Snyder & C. Ford (Eds.), *Coping with negative life events: Clinical and social psychological perspectives* (pp. 351-382). New York: Plenum.

Jenkins, C. D., Stanton, B., Savageau, J. A., Delinger, P., & Klein, M. D. (1983). Coronary artery bypass surgery: Physical, psychological, social, and economic outcomes six months later. *Journal of the American Medical Association, 250,* 782-788.

Joseph, S., Williams, R., & Yule, W. (1993). Changes in outlook following disaster: The preliminary development of a measure to assess positive and negative responses. *Journal of Traumatic Stress, 6,* 271-279.

Kahana, E., & Kinney, J. (1991). Understanding caregiving interventions in the context of the stress model. In R. F. Young & E. A. Olson (Eds.), *Health, illness, and disability in later life: Practice issues and interventions* (pp. 122-142). Newbury Park, CA: Sage.

Kamarck, T. W., Manuck, S. B., & Jennings, J. R. (1990). Social support reduces cardiovascular reactivity to psychological challenge: A laboratory model. *Psychosomatic Medicine, 52,* 42-58.

Kaplan, H. B. (1991). Social psychology of the immune system: A conceptual framework and review of the literature. *Social Science and Medicine, 33,* 909-923.

Kast, V. (1990). *The creative leap: Psychological transformation through crisis* (D. Whitcher, Trans.). Wilmette, IL: Chiron. (Original work published 1987)

Keller, H. (1968). *Midstream: My later life.* New York: Greenwood.

Kelly, G. A. (1955). *The psychology of personal constructs* (Vol. 1). New York: Norton.

Kelly, H. A. (1993). *Ideas and forms of tragedy from Aristotle to the Middle Ages.* Cambridge, UK: Cambridge University Press.

Kendall-Tackett, K. A., Williams, L. M., & Finkelhor, D. (1993). Impact of sexual abuse on children: A review and synthesis of recent empirical studies. *Psychological Bulletin, 113,* 164-180.

Kiecolt-Glaser, J. K., & Glaser, R. (1989). Psychoneuroimmunology: Past, present, and future. *Health Psychology, 8,* 677-682.

Kierkegaard, S. (1983). *Fear and trembling.* (H. V. Long & E. H. Long, Trans.). Princeton, NJ: Princeton University Press.

Kilpatrick, D. G., Veronen, L. J., & Best, C. L. (1985). Factors predicting psychological distress among rape victims. In C. R. Figley (Ed.), *Trauma and its wake: The study and treatment of post-traumatic stress disorder* (Vol. 1, pp. 113-141). New York: Brunner/Mazel.

Klass, D. (1986-1987). Marriage and divorce among bereaved parents in a self-help group. *Omega, 17,* 237-249.

Klein, W. M., & Kunda, Z. (1993). Maintaining self-serving social comparisons: Biased reconstruction of one's past behaviors. *Personality and Social Psychology Bulletin, 19,* 732-739.

Kobasa, S. C. (1979). Stressful life events, personality, and health: An inquiry into hardiness. *Journal of Personality and Social Psychology, 37,* 1-11.

Kobasa, S. C., Maddi, S. R., Puccetti, M. C., & Zola, M. A. (1985). Effectiveness of hardiness, exercise and social support as resources against illness. *Journal of Psychosomatic Research, 29,* 525-533.

Koenig, H. G., George, L. K., & Siegler, I. C. (1988). The use of religion and other emotion-regulating coping strategies among older adults. *Gerontologist, 28,* 303-310.

Komp, D. M. (1993). *A child shall lead them: Lessons in hope from children with cancer.* Grand Rapids, MI: Zondervan.

Kramer, D. A. (1990). Conceptualizing wisdom: The primacy of affect-cognition relations. In R. J. Sternberg (Ed.), *Wisdom: Its nature, origins, and development* (pp. 279-313). Cambridge, UK: Cambridge University Press.

Krementz, J. (1983). *How it feels when a parent dies.* New York: Knopf.

Krook, D. (1969). *Elements of tragedy.* New Haven, CT: Yale University Press.

Krystal, H. (1988). *Integration and self-healing: Affect, trauma, alexithymia.* Hillsdale, NJ: Analytic Press.

Kulik, J. A., & Mahler, H. I. M. (1993). Emotional support as a moderator of adjustment and compliance after coronary artery bypass surgery: A longitudinal study. *Journal of Behavioral Medicine, 16,* 45-63.

Kushner, H. S. (1981). *When bad things happen to good people.* New York: Avon.

Lagrande, L. E. (1988). *Changing patterns of human existence: Assumptions, beliefs, and coping with the stress of change.* Springfield, IL: Charles C Thomas.

Langer, E. J., & Rodin, J. (1976). The effects of choice and enhanced personal responsibility for the aged: A field experiment in an institutional setting. *Journal of Personality and Social Psychology, 34,* 191-198.

Lauer, R. H., & Lauer, J. C. (1988). *Watersheds: Mastering life's unpredictable crises.* New York: Ivy Books.

Lazarus, R., & Folkman, S. (1984). *Stress, appraisal and coping.* New York: Springer.

Leder, D. (1984-1985). Toward a phenomenology of pain. *Review of Existential Psychology and Psychiatry, 19,* 255-266.

Lehman, D. R., Davis, C. G., Delongis, A., Wortman, C., Bluck, S., Mandel, D. R., & Ellard, J. H. (1993). Positive and negative life changes following bereavement and their relations to adjustment. *Journal of Social and Clinical Psychology, 12,* 90-112.

Lehman, D. R., Ellard, J. H., & Wortman, C. B. (1986). Social support for the bereaved: Recipients' and providers' perspectives on what is helpful. *Journal of Consulting and Clinical Psychology, 54,* 438-446.

Lehman, D. R., Lang, E. L., Wortman, C. B., & Sorenson, S. B. (1989). Long-term effects of sudden bereavement: Marital and parent-child relationships and children's reactions. *Journal of Family Psychology, 2,* 344-367.

Lehman, D. R., Wortman, C. B., & Williams, A. F. (1987). Long-term effects of losing a spouse or child in a motor vehicle crash. *Journal of Personality and Social Psychology, 52,* 218-231.

Levy, S. M. (1985). *Behavior and cancer.* San Francisco: Jossey-Bass.

Lewis, C. S. (1963). *A grief observed.* New York: Seabury Press.

Lifton, R. J. (1993). *The protean self: Human resilience in an age of fragmentation.* New York: Basic Books.

Lincoln, Y., & Guba, E. (1985). *Naturalistic inquiry.* Beverly Hills, CA: Sage.

Lipowski, Z. J. (1970). Physical illness, the individual and the coping process. *Psychiatry in Medicine, 1,* 91-102.

Little, D. (1989). Human suffering in comparative perspective. In R. Taylor & J. Watson (Eds.), *They shall not hurt* (pp. 53-72). Boulder: Colorado Associated University Press.

Lopata, H. Z. (1973). Self-identity in marriage and widowhood. *Sociological Quarterly, 14,* 407-418.

Lund, D. A., Caserta, M. S., & Dimond, M. (1993). The course of spousal bereavement in later life. In M. S. Stroebe, W. Stroebe, & R. O. Hansson (Eds.), *Handbook of bereavement: Theory, research, and intervention* (pp. 240-254). Cambridge, UK: Cambridge University Press.

Lupfer, M. B., Brock, K. F., & DePaola, S. J. (1992). The use of secular and religious attributions to explain everyday behavior. *Journal for the Scientific Study of Religion, 31,* 486-503.

Maddi, S. R., Bartone, P. T., & Puccetti, M. C. (1987). Stressful events are indeed a factor in physical illness: Reply to Schroeder and Costa (1984). *Journal of Personality and Social Psychology, 52,* 833-843.

Mahoney, M. J. (1991). *Human change processes.* New York: Basic Books.

Malinak, D. P., Hoyt, M. F., & Patterson, V. (1979). Adults' reactions to the death of a parent. *American Journal of Psychiatry, 136,* 1152-1156.

Malinovsky-Rummell, R., & Hansen, D. J. (1993). Long-term consequences of childhood physical abuse. *Psychological Bulletin, 114,* 68-79.

Manning, M. R., Williams, R. F., & Wolfe, D. M. (1988). Hardiness and the relationship between stressors and outcomes. *Work and Stress, 2,* 205-216.

Martin, L. L., & Tesser, A. (1989). Toward a motivational and structural theory of ruminative thought. In J. S. Uleman & J. A. Bargh (Eds.), *Unintended thought* (pp. 306-326). New York: Guilford.

Martin, L. L., Tesser, A., & McIntosh, W. D. (1993). Wanting but not having: The effects of unattained goals on thoughts and feelings. In D. M. Wegner & J. W. Pennebaker (Eds.), *Handbook of mental control* (pp. 552-572). Englewood Cliffs, NJ: Prentice Hall.

Matlin, M., & Stang, D. (1978). *The Pollyanna principle: Selectivity in language, memory, and thought.* Cambridge, MA: Schenkman.

Maton, K. (1989). The stress-buffering role of spiritual support: Cross-sectional and prospective investigations. *Journal for the Scientific Study of Religion, 28,* 310-323.

May, R. (1981). *Freedom and destiny.* New York: Norton.

McAdams, D. P. (1989). The development of a narrative identity. In D. M. Buss & N. Cantor (Eds.), *Personality psychology: Recent trends and emerging directions* (pp. 160-174). New York: Springer-Verlag.

McAdams, D. P. (1993). *The stories we live by: Personal myths and the making of the self.* New York: Morrow.

McCann, I. L., & Pearlman, L. A. (1990). *Psychological trauma and the adult survivor: Theory, therapy, and transformation.* New York: Brunner/Mazel.

McCann, I. L., Sakheim, D. K., & Abrahamson, D. J. (1988). Trauma and victimization: A model of psychological adaptation. *Counseling Psychologist, 16,* 531-594.

McCrae, R. R., & Costa, P. T., Jr. (1993). Psychological resilience among widowed men and women: A 10-year follow-up of a national sample. In M. S. Stroebe, W. Stroebe, & R. O. Hansson (Eds.), *Handbook of bereavement: Theory, research and intervention* (pp. 196-207). Cambridge, UK: Cambridge University Press.

McIntosh, D. N. (1991, August). Religion as schema: Implications for the relation between religion and coping. In P. C. Hill (Chair), *Promising cognitive models for an empirical psychology of religion.* Symposium conducted at the annual meeting of the American Psychological Association, San Francisco.

Miles, L. (1965). (Ed.). *Saint Thomas More: A dialogue of comfort against tribulation.* Bloomington: Indiana University Press.

Miles, M. S., & Crandall, E. K. B. (1983). The search for meaning and its potential for affecting growth in bereaved parents. *Health Values, 7,* 19-23.

Miles, M. S., Demi, A. S., & Mostyn-Aker, P. (1984). Rescue workers' reactions following the Hyatt hotel disaster. *Death Education, 8,* 315-331.

Monahon, C. (1993). *Children and trauma: A parent's guide to helping children heal.* New York: Lexington Books.

Moran, C., & Britton, N. R. (1994). Emergency work experience and reaction to traumatic incidents. *Journal of Traumatic Stress, 7,* 575-585.

Moran, M. (1992, November 2). Basketball: This court jester knows the score. *New York Times,* p. C2.

Morgan, J. J., & Janoff-Bulman, R. (1992, August). *Positive self-complexity and reactions to traumatic events.* Paper presented at the annual meeting of the American Psychological Association, Washington, DC.

Moustakas, C. (1961). *Loneliness.* Englewood Cliffs, NJ: Prentice Hall.

Neeld, E. H. (1990). *Seven choices: Taking the steps to new life after losing someone you love.* New York: Delta.

Neimeyer, R. A. (1993). An appraisal of constructivist psychotherapies. *Journal of Consulting and Clinical Psychology, 61,* 221-234.

Nerken, I. R. (1993). Grief and the reflective self: Toward a clearer model of loss and growth. *Death Studies, 17,* 1-26.

Newman, J. S., & Pargament, K. I. (1990). The role of religion in the problem-solving process. *Review of Religious Research, 31,* 390-404.

Niebuhr, R. (1937). *Beyond tragedy: Essays on the Christian interpretation of history.* Freeport, NY: Books for Libraries Press.

Nietzsche, F. (1955). *Beyond good and evil* (M. Cowan, Trans.). Chicago: Henry Regnery.

Norris, F. H., Riad, J. K., & Kaniasty, K. (1993, August). *Reciprocity of enacted support and the preservation of resources following natural disaster.* Paper presented at the annual meeting of the American Psychological Association, Toronto.

Notarius, C. I., & Herrick, L. R. (1988). Listener response strategies to a distressed other. *Journal of Social and Personal Relationships, 5,* 97-108.

Ochberg, F. (Ed.). (1988). *Post-traumatic therapy and victims of violence.* New York: Brunner/Mazel.

O'Leary, A. (1990). Stress, emotion, and human immune function. *Psychological Bulletin, 108,* 363-382.

Osborne, J. W., & Baldwin, J. R. (1982). Psychotherapy: From one state of illusion to another? *Psychotherapy: Theory, Research, and Practice, 19,* 266-275.

Paolucci, A., & Paolucci, H. (1962). *Hegel on tragedy.* New York: Harper Torchbooks.

Pargament, K. (1990). God help me: Toward a theoretical framework of coping for the psychology of religion. *Research in the Social Scientific Study of Religion, 2,* 195-224.

Pargament, K. I., Falgout, K., Reilly, B., Ensing, D. S., Olsen, H., Van der Meulen, K., & Warren, R. (1991). *God help me (1): Religious coping efforts as predictors of the outcomes to significant life events.* Unpublished manuscript, Bowling Green State University.

Pargament, K. I., Kennell, J., Hathaway, W., Grevengoed, N., Newman, J., & Jones, W. (1988). Religion and the problem-solving process: Three styles of coping. *Journal for the Scientific Study of Religion, 27,* 90-104.

Pargament, K. I., Royster, B. J. T., Albert, M., Crowe, P., Cullman, E. P., Holley, R., Schaefer, D., Sytniak, M., & Wood, M. (1990, August). *A qualitative approach to the study of religion and coping: Four tentative conclusions.* Paper presented at the annual meeting of the American Psychological Association, Boston.

Park, C. L., & Cohen, L. H. (1993). Religious and nonreligious coping with the death of a friend. *Cognitive Therapy and Research, 17,* 561-577.

Park, C. L., Cohen, L., & Murch, R. (in press). Assessment and prediction of stress-related growth. *Journal of Personality.*

Parkes, C. M. (1971). Psycho-social transitions: A field for study. *Social Science and Medicine, 5,* 101-115.

Patterson, J. M. (1989). Illness beliefs as a factor in patient-spouse adaptation to treatment for coronary artery disease. *Family Systems Medicine, 7,* 428-442.

Pennebaker, J. W. (1990). *Opening up: The healing power of confiding in others.* New York: Morrow.

Pennebaker, J. W., Kiecolt-Glaser, J. K., & Glaser, R. (1988). Disclosure of traumas and immune function: Health implications for psychotherapy. *Journal of Consulting and Clinical Psychology, 56,* 239-245.

Perloff, L. S. (1983). Perceptions of vulnerability to victimization. *Journal of Social Issues, 39,* 41-61.

Perloff, L. S., & Fetzer, B. K. (1986). Self-other judgements and perceived vulnerability to victimization. *Journal of Personality and Social Psychology, 50,* 502-510.

Plunkett, J. W., Schaefer, M., Kalter, N., Okla, K., & Schreier, K. (1986). Perceptions of quality of life following divorce: A study of children's prognostic thinking. *Psychiatry, 49,* 1-12.

Price, R. (1994). *A whole new life.* New York: Atheneum.

Quarantelli, E. L. (1985). An assessment of conflicting views on mental health: The consequences of traumatic events. In C. R. Figley (Ed.), *Trauma and its wake: The study and treatment of post-traumatic stress disorder* (Vol. 1, pp. 173-218). New York: Brunner/Mazel.

Raphael, B. (1986). *When disaster strikes.* New York: Basic Books.

Raphael, D.D. (1960). *The paradox of tragedy.* Bloomington: Indiana University Press.

Reiss, D. (1981). *The family's construction of reality.* Cambridge, MA: Harvard University Press.

Riessman, C. K. (1993). *Narrative analysis.* Newbury Park, CA: Sage.

Rorty, A. O. (Ed.). (1992). *Essays on Aristotle's Poetics.* Princeton, NJ: Princeton University Press.

Ross, M. (1989). Relation of implicit theories to the construction of personal histories. *Psychological Review, 96,* 341-357.

Rothbaum, F., Weisz, J. R., & Snyder, S. S. (1982). Changing the world and changing the self: A two-process model of perceived control. *Journal of Personality and Social Psychology, 42,* 5-37.

Rotter, J. B. (1954). *Social learning and clinical psychology.* Englewood Cliffs, NJ: Prentice Hall.

Rotter, J. B. (1966). Generalized expectancies for internal versus external control of reinforcement. *Psychological Monographs, 80,* 1-28.

Rubonis, A. V., & Bickman, L. (1991). Psychological impairment in the wake of disaster: The disaster-psychopathology relationship. *Psychological Bulletin, 109,* 384-399.

Rudestam, K. E. (1977). Physical and psychological responses to suicide in the family. *Journal of Consulting and Clinical Psychology, 45,* 162-170.

Russell, R. L., & van den Broek, P. (1992). Changing narrative schemas in psychotherapy. *Psychotherapy, 29,* 344-354.

Rutter, M. (1987). Psychosocial resilience and protective mechanisms. *American Journal of Orthopsychiatry, 57,* 316-331.

Rybash, J. M., Hoyer, W. J., & Roodin, P. A. (1986). *Adult cognition and aging: Developmental changes in processing, knowing and thinking.* New York: Pergamon.

Saigh, P. A. (Ed.). (1992). *Posttraumatic stress disorder: A behavioral approach to assessment and treatment.* Needham Heights, MA: Longwood.

Sanford, J. A. (1977). *Healing and wholeness.* New York: Paulist Press.

Sarbin, T. R. (Ed.). (1986). *Narrative psychology: The storied nature of human conduct.* New York: Praeger.

Schaefer, J. A., & Moos, R. H. (1992). Life crises and personal growth. In B. N. Carpenter (Ed.), *Personal coping: Theory, research, and application* (pp. 149-170). Westport, CT: Praeger.

Scheier, M. F., & Carver, C. S. (1985). Optimism, coping, and health: Assessment and implications of generalized outcome expectancies. *Health Psychology, 4,* 219-247.

Scheier, M. F., & Carver, C. S. (1987). Dispositional optimism and physical well-being: The influence of generalized outcome expectancies on health. *Journal of Personality, 55,* 169-210.

Scheier, M. F., & Carver, C. S. (1992). Effects of optimism on psychological and physical well-being: Theoretical overview and empirical update. *Cognitive Therapy and Research, 16,* 201-228.

Scheier, M. F., Magovern, G. J., Sr., Abbott, R. A., Matthews, K. A., Owens, J. F., Lefebvre, R. C., & Carver, C. S. (1989). Dispositional optimism and recovery from coronary artery bypass surgery: The beneficial effects on physical and psychological well-being. *Journal of Personality and Social Psychology, 57,* 1024-1040.

Scheier, M. F., Weintraub, J. K., & Carver, C. S. (1986). Coping with stress: Divergent strategies of optimists and pessimists. *Journal of Personality and Social Psychology, 51,* 1257-1264.

Schier, F. (1983). Tragedy and the community of sentiment. In P. Lamarque (Ed.), *Philosophy and fiction: Essays in literary aesthetics* (pp. 73-92). Aberdeen, Scotland: The University Press.

Schlesinger, B. (1982). Children's viewpoints of living in a one-parent family. *Journal of Divorce, 5,* 1-23.

Schnaier, J. A. (1986). A study of women Vietnam veterans and their mental health adjustment. In C. R. Figley (Ed.), *Trauma and its wake: Traumatic stress theory research and intervention* (Vol. 2, pp. 97-132). New York: Brunner/Mazel.

Schopenhauer, A. (1942). The wisdom of life. In T. B. Saunders (Ed. and Trans.), *Complete essays of Schopenhauer* (pp. 1-124). New York: Willey Book Co.

Schultz, R. (1980). Aging and control. In J. Garber & M. E. P. Seligman (Eds.), *Human helplessness: Theory and applications* (pp. 261-277). New York: Academic Press.

Schwartzberg, S. S. (1993). Struggling for meaning: How HIV-positive gay men make sense of AIDS. *Professional Psychology: Research & Practice, 24,* 483-490.

Schwartzberg, S. S., & Janoff-Bulman, R. (1991). Grief and the search for meaning: Exploring the assumptive worlds of bereaved college students. *Journal of Social and Clinical Psychology, 10,* 270-288.

Scott, R. B. Y. (1971). *The way of wisdom.* New York: Macmillan.

Seeman, M., & Evans, J. W. (1962). Alienation and learning in a hospital setting. *American Sociological Review, 27,* 772-783.

Selby, J. W., & Calhoun, L. G. (1980) Psychodidactics: An undervalued and under-developed treatment tool of psychological intervention. *Professional Psychology, 11,* 236-241.

Seligman, M. E. P. (1975). *Helplessness: On depression, development, and death.* San Francisco: Freeman.

Selye, H. (1950). *The physiology and pathology of exposure to stress.* Montreal: Acta.

Shafranske, E. P., & Malony, H. N. (1990). Clinical psychologists' religious and spiritual orientations and their practice of psychotherapy. *Psychotherapy, 27,* 72-78.

Shay, J. (1994). *Achilles in Vietnam: Combat trauma and the undoing of character.* New York: Atheneum.

Shedler, J., Mayman, M., & Manis, M. (1993). The illusion of mental health. *American Psychologist, 48,* 1117-1131.

Shelton, R. R., Calhoun, L. G., & Tedeschi, R. G. (1994, August). *Significant life events: A qualitative study of narrative elements.* Paper presented at the annual meeting of the American Psychological Association, Los Angeles.

Shinn, R. L. (1986, January 1-8). Reinhold Niebuhr: A reverberating voice. *Christian Century,* pp. 15-17.

Shontz, F. C. (1975). *The psychological aspects of physical illness and disability.* New York: Macmillan.

Shore, J. H., Tatum, E. L., & Vollmer, W. M. (1986). Psychiatric reactions to disaster: The Mount St. Helens experience. *American Journal of Psychiatry, 143,* 590-595.

Shostrom, E. L. (1976). *Actualizing therapy: Foundations for a scientific ethic.* San Diego, CA: Edits Publishers.

Silver, R. C., Boon, C., & Stones, M. H. (1983). Searching for meaning in misfortune: Making sense of incest. *Journal of Social Issues, 39,* 81-102.

Silver, R. C., & Urbanowicz, A. (1990, August). A study of successful and unsuccessful support providers following bereavement. In K. Heller (Chair), *Understanding the factors responsible for support intervention success and failure.* Symposium conducted at the annual meeting of the American Psychological Association, Boston.

Silver, R. C., & Wortman, C. B. (1980). Coping with undesirable life events. In J. Garber & M. E. P. Seligman (Eds.), *Human helplessness: Theory and applications* (pp. 279-340). New York: Academic Press.

Singer, J. A., & Salovey, P. (1993). *The remembered self: Emotion and memory in personality.* New York: Free Press.

Singer, J. K. (1964). A guide to Job's encounter. In R. Breaktone (Ed.), *Job: A case study* (pp. 237-317). New York: Bookman.

Slaby, A. E. (1989). *Aftershock: Surviving the delayed effects of trauma, crisis and loss.* New York: Villard.

Sledge, W. H., Boydstun, J. A., & Rabe, A. J. (1980). Self-concept changes related to war captivity. *Archives of General Psychiatry, 37,* 430-443.

Smith, T. W., Houston, B. K., & Stucky, R. J. (1982). Positive evaluation as a strategy for coping with stress. *Journal of Social and Clinical Psychology, 1,* 193-208.

Smith, T. W., Pope, M. K., Rhodewalt, F., & Poulton, J. L. (1989). Optimism, neuroticism, coping, and symptom reports: An alternative interpretation of the life orientation test. *Journal of Personality and Social Psychology, 56,* 640-648.

Spilka, B. (1989). Functional and dysfunctional roles of religion: An attributional approach. *Journal of Psychology and Christianity, 8,* 5-15.

Stewart, A. J. (1982). The course of individual adaptation. *Journal of Personality and Social Psychology, 42,* 1100-1113.

Stotland, E. (1969). *The psychology of hope: An integration of experimental, clinical, and social approaches.* San Francisco: Jossey-Bass.

Strauss, A. (1987). *Qualitative analysis for social scientists.* Cambridge, UK: Cambridge University Press.

Strickland, B. R. (1989). Internal-external control expectancies: From contingency to creativity. *American Psychologist, 44,* 1-12.

Stroebe, M., Gergen, M. M., Gergen, K., & Stroebe, W. (1992). Broken hearts or broken bonds—Love and death in historical perspective. *American Psychologist, 47,* 1205-1212.

Stutman, S., & Baruch, R. (1992, August). A model for the process of fostering resilience. In H. Tomes (Chair), *The process of fostering resilience: Roles for psychologists and media.* Symposium conducted at the annual meeting of the American Psychological Association, Washington, DC.

Stutts, W., Calhoun, L. G., Tedeschi, R. G., & Cann, A. (1994, August). *Religion, assumptive worlds, and the aftermath of trauma: What changes?* Paper presented at the annual meeting of the American Psychological Association, Los Angeles.

Swann, W. B. (1983). Self-verification: Bringing social reality into harmony with the self. In J. Suls & A. G. Greenwald (Eds.), *Social psychological perspectives on the self* (Vol. 2, pp. 33-66). Hillsdale, NJ: Lawrence Erlbaum.

Swindle, R. W., Jr., Heller, K., & Lakey, B. (1988). A conceptual reorientation to the study of personality and stressful life events. In L. H. Cohen (Ed.), *Life events and psychological functioning: Theoretical and methodological issues* (pp. 237-268). Newbury Park, CA: Sage.

Tait, R., & Silver, R. C. (1989). Coming to terms with major negative life events. In J. S. Uleman & J. A. Bargh (Eds.), *Unintended thought* (pp. 351-382). New York: Guilford.

Taylor, S. E. (1983). Adjustment to threatening life events. *American Psychologist, 38,* 1161-1173.

Taylor, S. E. (1990). Health psychology—The science and the field. *American Psychologist, 45,* 40-50.

Taylor, S. E., & Brown, J. D. (1988). Illusion and well-being: A social psychological perspective on mental health. *Psychological Bulletin, 103,* 193-210.

Taylor, S. E., & Brown, J. D. (1994). Positive illusions and well-being revisited: Separating fact from fiction. *Psychological Bulletin, 116,* 21-27.

Taylor, S. E., Collins, R. L., Skokan, L. A., & Aspinwall, L. G. (1989). Maintaining positive illusions in the face of negative information: Getting the facts without letting them get to you. *Journal of Social and Clinical Psychology, 8,* 114-129.

Taylor, S. E., Falke, R. L., Mazel, R. M., & Hilsberg, B. L. (1988). Sources of satisfaction and dissatisfaction among members of cancer support groups. In B. H. Gottlieb (Ed.), *Marshaling social support* (pp. 187-208). Newbury Park, CA: Sage.

Taylor, S. E., Lichtman, R. R., & Wood, J. V. (1984). Attributions, beliefs in control, and adjustment to breast cancer. *Journal of Personality and Social Psychology, 46*, 489-502.

Taylor, S. E., Wayment, H. A., & Collins, M. A. (1993). Positive illusions and affect regulation. In D. M. Wegner & J. W. Pennebaker (Eds.), *Handbook of mental control* (pp. 325-434). Englewood Cliffs, NJ: Prentice Hall.

Taylor, S. E., Wood, J. V., & Lichtman, R. R. (1983). It could be worse: Selective evaluation as a response to victimization. *Journal of Social Issues, 39*, 19-40.

Taylor, V. (1977, October). Good news about disaster. *Psychology Today*, pp. 93-94, 124-126.

Tedeschi, R. G. (1989, August). The masculine gender role as impediment to rehabilitation. In G. Brooks (Chair), *Beyond the masculine mystique: Loosening male gender role bonds.* Symposium conducted at the annual meeting of the American Psychological Association, New Orleans, LA.

Tedeschi, R. G., & Calhoun, L. G. (1988, August). *Perceived benefits in coping with physical handicaps.* Paper presented at the annual meeting of the American Psychological Association, Atlanta.

Tedeschi, R. G., & Calhoun, L. G. (1991). Perceiving benefits in traumatic events: Some issues for practicing psychologists. *Journal of Training & Practice in Professional Psychology, 5*, 45-52.

Tedeschi, R. G., & Calhoun, L. G. (1993). Using the support group to respond to the isolation of bereavement. *Journal of Mental Health Counseling, 15*, 47-54.

Tedeschi, R. G., & Calhoun, L. G. (in press). The Post Traumatic Growth Inventory: Measuring the positive legacy of trauma. *Journal of Traumatic Stress.*

Tedeschi, R. G., Calhoun, L. G., & Gross, B. J. (1993, August). *Construing benefits from negative events: An examination of personality variables.* Paper presented at the annual meeting of the American Psychological Association, Toronto.

Tedeschi, R. G., Calhoun, L. G., & Page, L. (1992, August). *Possibilities for growth in positive and negative life events.* Paper presented at the annual meeting of the American Psychological Association, Washington, DC.

Tennen, H., & Affleck, G. (1990). Blaming others for threatening events. *Psychological Bulletin, 108*, 209-232.

Thoits, P. A. (1991). Gender differences in coping. In J. Eckenrode (Ed.), *The social context of coping* (pp. 107-138). New York: Plenum.

Thomas, G. (1978). Transforming the tragic into the creative. In H. J. Young (Ed.), *Preaching on suffering and a God of love* (pp. 18-21). Philadelphia: Fortress Press.

Thomas, L. E., DiGiulio, R. C., & Sheehan, N. W. (1991). Identifying loss and psychological crisis in widowhood. *International Journal of Aging and Human Development, 26*, 279-295.

Thompson, S. C. (1981). Will it hurt less if I can control it? A complex answer to a simple question. *Psychological Bulletin, 90*, 89-101.

Thompson, S. C. (1985). Finding positive meaning in a stressful event and coping. *Basic and Applied Social Psychology, 6*, 279-295.

Thompson, S. C., & Janigian, A. S. (1988). Life schemes: A framework for understanding the search for meaning. *Journal of Social and Clinical Psychology, 7*, 260-280.

Tiger, L. (1979, January). Optimism: The biological roots of hope. *Psychology Today*, pp. 18-33.

Vaillant, G. E. (1977). *Adaptation to life*. Boston: Little, Brown.

van den Broek, P., & Thurlow, R. (1991). The role and structure of personal narratives. *Journal of Cognitive Psychotherapy, 5,* 257-274.

van der Kolk, B. A. (1986). *Psychological trauma*. Washington, DC: American Psychiatric Press.

Van der Wal, J. (1990). The aftermath of suicide: A review of empirical evidence. *Omega, 20,* 149-171.

Vash, C. L. (1981). *The psychology of disability*. New York: Springer.

Veronen, L. J., & Kilpatrick, D. G. (1983). Rape: A precursor of change. In E. J. Callahan & K. A. McCluskey (Eds.), *Life span developmental psychology: Nonnormative events* (pp. 167-191). San Diego, CA: Academic Press.

Viorst, J. (1986). *Necessary losses*. New York: Fawcett.

Wagner, K. G., & Calhoun, L. G. (1991). Perceptions of social support by suicide survivors and their social networks. *Omega, 23,* 61-73.

Wallerstein, J. S. (1986). Women after divorce: Preliminary report from a ten-year follow-up. *American Journal of Orthopsychiatry, 56,* 65-77.

Wallston, K. A., & Wallston, B. S. (1982). Who is responsible for your health? The construct of health locus of control. In G. S. Sanders & J. Suls (Eds.), *Social psychology of health and illness* (pp. 65-95). Hillsdale, NJ: Lawrence Erlbaum.

Waltz, M. (1986). Marital context and post-infarction quality of life: Is it social support or something more? *Social Science and Medicine, 22,* 791-805.

Waltz, M., & Bandura, B. (1988). Subjective health, intimacy, and perceived self-efficacy after heart attack: Predicting life quality five years afterwards. *Social Indicators Research, 20,* 303-332.

Wasch, H., & Kirsch, I. (1992, August). *Response expectancy and coping as predictors of dysphoric mood*. Paper presented at the annual meeting of the American Psychological Association, Washington, DC.

Weinstein, N. D. (1980). Unrealistic optimism about future life events. *Journal of Personality and Social Psychology, 39,* 806-823.

Weiss, R., & Parkes, C. M. (1983). *Recovery from bereavement*. New York: Basic Books.

Werner, E. E. (1984, November). Resilient children. *Young Children*, pp. 68-72.

Werner, E. E. (1989). High-risk children in young adulthood: A longitudinal study from birth to 32 years. *American Journal of Orthopsychiatry, 59,* 72-81.

Werner, E. E., & Smith, R. S. (1982). *Vulnerable but invincible: A longitudinal study of resilient children and youth*. New York: McGraw-Hill.

Wertheimer, A. (1991). *A special fear*. London: Routledge.

Whiteman, D. B. (1993). Holocaust survivors and escapees—Their strengths. *Psychotherapy, 30,* 443-451.

Wiebe, D. J. (1991). Hardiness and stress moderation: A test of proposed mechanisms. *Journal of Personality and Social Psychology, 60,* 89-99.

Wilkinson, C. B. (1983). Aftermath of disaster: The collapse of the Hyatt Regency Hotel skywalks. *American Journal of Psychiatry, 140,* 1134-1139.

Wills, T. A. (1987). Downward comparison as a coping mechanism. In C. R. Snyder & C. E. Ford (Eds.), *Coping with negative life events: Clinical and social psychological perspectives* (pp. 243-268). New York: Plenum.

Wilson, J. P. (1989). *Trauma, transformation, and healing: An integrative approach to theory, research, and post-traumatic therapy*. New York: Brunner/Mazel.

Wilson, S. R., & Spencer, R. C. (1990). Intense personal experiences: Subjective effects, interpretations, and after-effects. *Journal of Clinical Psychology, 46,* 565-573.

Wolin, S. J., & Wolin, S. (1993). *The resilient self: How survivors of troubled families rise above adversity.* New York: Villard.

Wood, J. V., Taylor, S. E., & Lichtman, R. R. (1985). Social comparison in adjustment to breast cancer. *Journal of Personality and Social Psychology, 49,* 1169-1183.

Wortman, C. B., & Lehman, D. R. (1985). Reactions to victims of life crises. In I. G. Sarason & B. R. Sarason (Eds.), *Social support: Theory, research, and applications* (pp. 463-489). Dordrecht, Netherlands: Martinus Nijhoff.

Wortman, C. B., & Silver, R. C. (1989). The myths of coping with loss. *Journal of Consulting and Clinical Psychology, 57,* 349-357.

Wortman, C. B., & Silver, R. C. (1990). Successful mastery of bereavement and widowhood: A life-course perspective. In P. B. Baltes & M. M. Baltes (Eds.), *Successful aging* (pp. 225-264). Cambridge, UK: Cambridge University Press.

Wuthnow, R. (1991). *Acts of compassion: Caring for others and helping ourselves.* Princeton, NJ: Princeton University Press.

Wuthnow, R. (1992). *Rediscovering the sacred.* Grand Rapids, MI: William B. Eerdmans.

Wuthnow, R. (1994). *Sharing the journey: Support groups and America's new quest for community.* New York: Free Press.

Younkin, S. L. (1992, August). *Psychological hardiness in stress resistance versus vulnerability: A reconceptualization.* Paper presented at the annual meeting of the American Psychological Association, Washington, DC.

Zemore, R., & Shepel, L. F. (1989). The effects of breast cancer and mastectomy on emotional support and adjustment. *Social Science and Medicine, 28,* 19-27.

INDEX

ABOUT THE AUTHORS

Richard G. Tedeschi is Associate Professor of Psychology at the University of North Carolina at Charlotte and a practicing clinical psychologist. He is the author of articles on coping and growth in response to trauma, with bereavement being a particular area of study. He has been interested in the process of mutual support as a facilitator of parental and sibling bereavement support groups for many years. His university teaching has focused on the psychology of personality and on clinical training and supervision, especially integrative therapy techniques and clinician responses to client trauma. His nonprofessional time is taken up with tending to his patch of land in the country.

Lawrence G. Calhoun is Professor of Psychology at the University of North Carolina at Charlotte and a practicing clinical psychologist. He is the coauthor of *Dealing With Crisis* (1976), *Psychology and Human Reproduction* (1980), and numerous scholarly articles, and he is currently on the editorial board of *Omega—Journal of Death and Dying*. His scholarly activities have focused on the responses of persons encountering significant life crises and on the social responses of others to the individuals directly affected by trauma. He has taught both undergraduate and graduate courses in a variety of applied areas, and his clinical work is focused on adults facing depression and anxiety or coping with highly challenging life circumstances. His nonprofessional interests include reading, pickup games of basketball, and, as a Brazilian-born American, a fanatical devotion to World Cup soccer.